The No-Bullying Program

Preventing Bully/Victim Violence at School

Teacher's Manual For Kindergarten and Grade 1

James Bitney—Curriculum Writer

Beverly B. Title, Ph.D.—Program Developer

JOHNSON INSTITUTE®

Minneapolis

Acknowledgment

The contents of this book are based on the No-Bullying Curriculum model originally developed for the St. Vrain Valley School District, Longmont, Colorado, by Beverly B. Title, with assistance from Lisa Anderson-Goebel, Vivian Bray, K.G. Campanella-Green, Ted Goodwin, Karen Greene, Elizabeth Martinson, Mike O'Connell, and Peggy Stortz.

The Bullying Behavior Chart was developed by Beverly B. Title, Ph.D.; Severance Kelly, M.D.; Louis Krupnik, Ph.D.; Joseph Matthews, M.S.W.; Kendra Bartley, M.A.

Curriculum consultation was provided by Peggy O'Connell.

The No-Bullying Program: Preventing Bully/Victim Violence at School
Teacher's Manual for Kindergarten and Grade 1

James Bitney, Curriculum Writer
Beverly B. Title, Ph.D., Program Developer

Johnson Institute
7205 Ohms Lane
Minneapolis, Minnesota 55439-2159
612-831-1630 or 800-231-5165

ISBN 1-56246-119-2

Logo design: Diana Garcia
Cover and text design: Crombie Design
Artwork by Sally Brewer Lawrence
Printed in the United States of America

96 97 98 99 / 5 4 3 2 1

Contents

INTRODUCTION
School Zones—Danger Zones

In 1991, 25,000 people were murdered in the United States. During that same year, there were over 67 million handguns in the United States. Sadly, many of the most heavily armed are young people. One official described the arming of America's teenagers as a real "arms race" in which "no one wants to be left behind." Many schools list weapons on campus as one of their top concerns. An eighth grader in a Connecticut junior high school was suspended for refusing to remove his hat. The next day, he came to school with an assault rifle, killed the janitor and wounded the principal and the school secretary.

A thirteen year old in Florida threatened to torture and kill his social studies teacher after receiving a poor grade on a test. When the boy was arrested, he had two pistols, a box of bullets, and a switchblade.

After losing a very close foot race, an eighth-grade girl shot the winner, a classmate, in the leg, claiming, "She cheated."

Violence threatens the fiber of our education system both for teachers and for students. In some schools, gun fights have replaced fist fights and "bullet drills" have replaced fire drills. Guns aren't the only weapons at school. Students have been caught with knives, razors, even bombs. Students say they carry weapons for protection. In 1991, over 3 million young people became the victims of violent crime at school.

Teachers do not fare much better than students. A report from the National Education Association indicates that every month of the school year 12% of teachers will have something stolen, 6,000 will have something taken from them forcefully, 120,000 will be threatened, 5,200 will be attacked, and 19% of those attacked will require medical attention.

Violence: A Definition

These startling statistics point out that too many students and teachers are unsafe in their own schools. Too many use violence, witness violence, or are victims of violence. Unfortunately, violence means different things to different people. That is why the Johnson Institute has sought to define violence as:

> **Any word, look, sign, or act that inflicts or threatens to inflict physical or emotional injury or discomfort upon another person's body, feelings, or possessions.**

Violence: A Delineation

Basically, there are two types of violence: peer violence and bully/victim violence.

- Peer violence is defined as acts of violence stemming from disagreements, misunderstandings, or conflicting desires among students who are equally matched in strength and power.

- Bully/victim violence involves an imbalance of power and strength between students; bully/victim violence occurs whenever a student intentionally, repeatedly, and over time inflicts or threatens to inflict physical or emotional injury or discomfort on another's body, feelings, or possessions.

Both kinds must be dealt with to make our schools safe.

Dealing with Bully/Victim Violence: The No-Bullying Program

Schools can successfully deal with the problem of peer violence by helping children grow in social skills: communication, feeling processing, problem solving, conflict management, and conflict mediation. Unfortunately, schools have not been so successful in dealing with bully/victim violence.

The No-Bullying Program has been designed to provide a research-based, educational model to deal with bully/victim violence in the school. Research has clearly shown that bullies do not respond to social skill work. Bullies do not care that what they are doing is creating problems for others. In fact, they generally enjoy the results of their bullying behavior. *The No-Bullying Program* offers schools a plan for dealing with bullies and bully/victim violence.

Approximately 15 % of any school population are bullies or victims of bullies, which means that 85% of the school population are relatively uninvolved in bullying behaviors. To end bullying, the *No-Bullying Program* engages the help of that 85% by:

- Clearly defining what is and what is not bullying

- Creating empathy for the victims of bullying

- Teaching students when and how to report bullying

- Establishing clear consequences for bullying that are strictly enforced by everyone in the school

To assure the help of that 85%, the *No-Bullying Program* also insists that *all adults* in the school take more proactive roles in dealing with bullies and their victims. Research has shown that adult intervention is crucial to ending bully/victim violence. Once children realize that reporting bullying to an adult will result in immediate intervention and action (consequences), they feel secure in becoming proactive in ending bullying themselves.

Prior to meeting with the children, you have met with *all* school staff and support staff to:

- overview *The No-Bullying Program* in its entirety; review research and correct misinformation about bullying: its perpetrators and its victims

- learn how to stop enabling bullying behavior

- agree on a school-wide policy of no-entitlement and no-tolerance with regard to bullying behaviors

- learn intervention strategies with regard to bullying behaviors

- create support networks with community leaders and service providers, professionals in the areas of violence and domestic abuse, law enforcement officials, student leaders, and parent advisory group leaders or members

- establish a procedure enabling the children to feel safe when reporting bullying

- set and commit to the consistent enforcement of school-wide consequences for bullying behaviors.

Now, as a teacher, your role in the project is to lead the children through an exciting educational process designed to empower them to end bullying in their school and to make it a "Safe Zone" for learning.

How to Use This Manual

This *Teacher's Manual* offers you material and detailed guidance to lead kindergartners and first graders through eight 25- to 30-minute sessions of interactive learning. You may lengthen or shorten the session time, depending on the deletion or addition of an activity and your particular teaching style.

Aims of the Program

This program aims to teach strategically formulated awarenesses and skills that are designed to help the children:

- understand the *No-Bullying Program*

- define bullying, share ideas about bully/victim problems, and heighten their awareness of these problems

- define and enumerate bullying behaviors

- better understand and deal with feelings

- learn to deal with angry feelings and avoid bullying behaviors

- develop empathy for the victims of bullying

- recognize the distinction between tattling and telling in order to get help in a bullying situation

- learn the school-wide consequences for engaging in bullying behaviors

Learning Strategies

The *No-Bullying Program* incorporates a variety of strategies to help you facilitate learning. These strategies include:

- Kinesthetic learning tactics

- Brainstorming

- Storytelling

- Drama and role playing

- Group discussion

- Teaching Masters

- Singing

Kinesthetic Learning Tactics

An ancient Oriental proverb states: "Tell me, I'll forget. Show me, I may remember. But involve me, and I'll understand." Put simply, kinesthetic learning techniques *involve* the children. Using these techniques allows you to appeal to more than one sense of the learner. They even allow you to get learners moving, so that body muscles may respond to the learning stimuli.

When the children hear you say something and, at the same time, see some information you've printed on the board or newsprint, they retain more of what you're saying. As you teach, then, frequently write out words and terms as you say them. Likewise, capture attention by using sight as well as hearing. If you write a word or term, circle, star, box, underline, or check it if you refer to it a second or third time. Draw lines and arrows to connect words—to draw connections between terms. Consider using different colored chalk or markers to show relationships or connections between words and terms. This does more than add color; it makes relationships stand out.

Avail yourself of every opportunity to get the children on their feet, raise their hands, turn in their seats. Encourage them to use all their senses as they learn.

Brainstorming

Brainstorming allows everyone to speak quickly and briefly and puts the burden of knowledge on no one person. Brainstorming is proof of the adage that "All of us are smarter than any one of us." Brainstorming is an activity that's easy to do and with which almost all children are comfortable, since every brainstorming response or idea is an acceptable one.

When the children brainstorm, list their responses (or words that describe them) on the board or newsprint, but don't add your comments; for example: "Good!" "Just what I was thinking." "I don't see how that fits, but I'll write it down anyway." "Do you really mean that?" Your comments, either positive or negative, can prevent some children from saying anything at all or can embarrass others. Be aware that as the children brainstorm, a type of synergism takes place. Initial responses elicit new responses that pull together many ideas into one. This synergism tends to energize the children and make them eager to join in.

When brainstorming, be wary of searching for "the right response" and then stopping the brainstorming once somebody gives it. Instead, set a time limit for brainstorming and get all the responses you can during that time. Or simply end the brainstorming when the children stop coming up with ideas.

Finally, brainstorming helps children realize that they already know a great deal, that the answers to questions they may have already lie within them. Thus, brainstorming helps the children value themselves and appreciate that you value them.

Storytelling

"Once upon a time." These are magic words. Stories create worlds beyond the senses for children. Dragons and witches live there, but so do lords and ladies. In stories, children can pretend they are animals in a jungle, knights in shining armor, or even all grown up. Stories entertain, inform, instruct, heighten celebration, expose listeners to other people and other worlds, engage feelings and arouse empathy, and often become ways to remember the deepest meanings of human experience. Stories open the minds of children and can even lead them to living happily ever after.

This level of *The No-Bullying Program* employs a number of stories for use with the children. Their success depends a lot on you. When you are preparing to share one of the stories with the children, read through it carefully on your own and take time to think about it in light of the session's objectives. Identify for yourself the story's basic structure—its characters and setting, the main events in the plot, the climax to which it builds, the conclusion. When you actually share the story with the children, live the story; read it as if you were living it. Express emotion through facial expression, gestures, and tone of voice. Utilize suggested visual aids (pictures, puppets, etc.). Make frequent eye contact with the children.

Recognizing that kindergartners and first graders have short attention spans, also recognize that they have a great need for sharing. Recognize, however, that if a story is interrupted, it loses its overall impact. Therefore, rather than allowing children to intrude on a story, ask them to hold their questions or comments until the story is ended. Only then, provide time for sharing.

During storytelling, allow the children to sit closely and comfortably around you. When you use visual aids, however, don't let children block one another's view. When discussing a story—even when using discussion questions provided in this manual for leading such discussion—try not to turn the discussion into a "test." The influence of a story is often subtle and needs time to work within the children.

Drama and Role Playing

In drama (skits) and role playing, children assume various characters and create roles. During role play, they may explore situations, identify problems, resolve conflicts, and create solutions. In other words, they deal with real-life matters in a safe situation. They can *safely* experience a whole range of emotions as they identify with characters and roles and work toward creative solutions. These activities can provide insights for the children that simple discussion cannot.

At the conclusion of a drama (skit) or role play, always offer those who took part the opportunity to express and process their feelings. Likewise, offer the observers the chance to share their observations and perceptions.

Group Discussion

In group discussion a synergy that is more than just the sum of the number of children in the group can result from their talking together and sharing ideas. The sum becomes more than the addition of its parts.

Teaching Masters

This level of the *No-Bullying Program* provides you with 18 Teaching Masters (see pages 73–92), which you can reproduce, and most of which serve as handouts for the children to use as worksheets to explore the key concepts of a particular session.

> **Note:** Depending on when this program is presented (early or late in the school year), kindergartners and first graders may have difficulty reading the text on the Teaching Masters as well as any text you may print on the board or newsprint while leading the sessions. Be sure, then, to point out and read aloud all written words to the children.

Singing

This level of *The No-Bullying Program* uses singing within the concluding activity of each session. It does so, first of all, because children love singing. Moreover, singing also adds a spirit of celebration, joy, and excitement to learning. At this age, the children learn to sing by listening and repeating a song line by line (rote singing). If you sing a song through and then repeat it phrase by phrase and have the children sing it after you, they will be able to sing the complete song. The song used in this level of *The No-Bullying Program* is set to a well-known melody. Words and musical notation for the song can be found on page 92, as well as in each session.

> **Note:** If you do not consider yourself a singer and/or are uncomfortable singing, ask someone to make you a tape recording that you can use with the children.

Understanding the Five- to Six-year-old Child

For the most part, the following characteristics—all of which are normal—are exhibited by the five- to six-year-old child. He or she:

- trusts adults and older children

- seeks and needs adult encouragement and reassurance

- is very dependent on parents for support, direction, approval, and love

- is very sensitive to both praise and criticism

- knows right from wrong, but only by being told so by adults

- is unsure of how he or she is behaving (e.g., evidence questions like, "Teacher, was I good today?")

- is interested in the work, concerns, and opinions of parents

- learns in the concrete; that is, by doing; thus, he or she needs and enjoys hands-on learning and repetition

- is beginning to enjoy joining with peers for play and learning activities

- has a clear sex identity and prefers to be with his or her own sex

- has a brief attention span; needs a variety of activities to stimulate interest

- requires a stable, consistent environment for learning

- possesses a rich dream and fantasy life and likes to explore them as much as the real world

- is often moved by images and fantasies, but can also be terrified by frightening or destructive images

- is often inconsistent in behavior

- possesses a sense of justice and fairness based on reciprocity ("If I do well, I will be rewarded. If I do bad, I will be punished.")

- is often not aware of the perspective or feelings of others

- exhibits shyness around unfamiliar people

- can feel jealousy toward siblings and friends

- still has occasional outbursts of temper and inappropriate behavior

- is not always able to identify, own, and express feelings adequately or suitably

Session Components

- **Aim** states the overall goal of the session.

- **Objectives** lists the learning outcomes of the session.

- **Materials** catalogues all the teaching devices necessary to present the session.

- **Preparing for the Session** contains directions for all the pre-session arrangements necessary to present the session.

- **Background for the Teacher** includes pertinent information:

  — to help you set the educational content in context;

  — to provide you with added information for personal growth;

  — to give you new data necessary to present the session with the greatest success.

- **Session Plan** includes the specific steps or directions for presenting the session. Each Session Plan is composed of three parts: *Beginning the Session, Leading the Session,* and *Concluding the Session.*

— *Beginning the Session* serves to welcome and gather the children, unite them as a group, review previous learning, and get them ready to work and share together.

— *Leading the Session* includes learning activities, discussions, exercises, drama or role play, as well as other educational processes, presented in a clear, step-by-step design that enables you to guide the children through the session.

— *Concluding the Session*, which remains relatively the same for every session, includes activities that serve to affirm the children in what they learned during the session and to help them commit themselves to No-bullying both as individuals and as a school community.

Finally, some of the plans include an Optional Activity, which you may choose to use to replace an activity in the plan, to enhance the plan, or to extend the session.

This session plan format strives to give the children a total experience that is structured but hospitable, instructive but creative, and challenging but supportive. Because the format remains constant for each session, it also meets the needs of at-risk children for structure, stability, consistency, and enjoyment. You may use the plans with confidence.

Session 1

Aim

To introduce the *No-Bullying Program* to the children

Objectives

By the end of the session, the children will

- recognize and understand the No-Bullying logo

- begin to identify bullying and its effects

- appreciate that their school is committed to ending bullying

Materials

- copy of the No-Bullying logo poster (Teaching Master 1)

- newsprint and marker

- cut-outs of the No-Bullying logos (Teaching Master 2)

- posterboard backing cut-outs

- colored markers or crayons, glue sticks or paste

- paper punch

- yarn

- optional: *Being Bullied* by Kate Perry and Charlotte Firmin (see page 95)

Preparing for the Session

Carefully read over the session plan in advance. Make a copy of the No-Bullying logo poster (Teaching Master 1) to be used throughout the sessions.

Make copies of the No-Bullying logos (Teaching Master 2), enough so that each child can have his or her own logo. Pre-cut the logos from the sheets. Using one of the logos as a guide, from posterboard, cut out backing for each of the logos. Have a paper punch at hand. Have a pre-cut, 18-inch length of yarn available for each child.

Review the song, "No Bullying" (see Step 7 below), which is sung to the tune of "Row, Row, Row Your Boat," and will be used to conclude each session. A larger version of the words and music may be found on page 92 of this manual. Likewise, familiarize yourself with the A.S.L. (American Sign Language) sign for "no/not" as illustrated in Step 7 in order to teach it to the children and to use it in the song.

Finally, if you choose to use the Optional Activity, make all necessary arrangements and adjustments to the Session Plan.

Background for the Teacher

It is important for you, as a teacher, to understand that bullying is not always obvious. It most often takes place in concealed areas. At school, bullying occurs where you're not present or where you can't see: in bathrooms, in hallways, on playground areas that are difficult to supervise, in empty classrooms, etc. Simply because you do not witness bullying behaviors does not mean they aren't taking place.

Session Plan

Beginning the Session

Gather the children in a circle. Join the circle yourself. Introduce yourself and offer your own words of welcome. Then, beginning with child on your right, go around the circle, having each child introduce himself or herself and then tell one thing that makes him or her feel safe at school.

Leading the Session

1. Display the copy of the No-Bullying Logo Poster. Ask the children what they think it may mean. Accept all replies and list them on a sheet of newsprint.

2. Drawing on the children's ideas, lead a discussion about the logo with the group. Encourage the children to share:

   • what types of things they think bullying children do

- what happens to children who bully others

- what happens to children who are being bullied

- how bullying affects their school.

Again, as you discuss, list children's ideas on newsprint.

> **Note:** Save the newsprint sheet for use in Step 4 below, and again in Sessions 2 and 3.

3. After the discussion, tell the children that they will be talking more about bullying behavior—about children taking unfair advantage of others—for the next few weeks. Point out that your school wants to help stop all bullying and getting hurt by bullying in your school. Then say:

> "In our class time together, we will learn how to help each other and how and when to tell a trusted adult about bullying. However, whenever we talk about bullying *in this class*, we will never call anyone by name who is bullying others or any child who is being bullied."

4. Drawing on their ideas from the discussion in Step 2, help the children express:

- why they think bullies do what they do.

- how they think a bully may feel.

- how they think being bullied might make them feel.

As the children get into talking about feelings, help them to avoid calling feelings "good" or "bad." Instead, encourage them to *name* feelings more specifically; for example, "sad," "angry," "frightened," "ashamed," etc. If the children have difficulty in naming feelings, invite them to show the feeling on their faces or with their bodies.

5. Tell the children that they will make their own No-Bullying medallions to wear. Distribute cut-outs of the No-Bullying logo and crayons or colored markers. Invite the children to choose any color they wish and to color the logo's circle and slash mark. Then pass out the posterboard backing cut-outs you prepared prior to the session and the glue sticks or paste. Direct the children to affix their colored logos to the posterboard backing.

6. When the children finish gluing, punch a hole in the top of their medallions, thread yarn through the hole, tie the yarn, and have the children

place their medallions around their necks. Encourage the children to wear their No-Bullying medallions at school.

Tell the group that everyone in your school—children and adults—will be working hard at stopping all bullying in school. Once again, assure the children that they will be learning ways to help one another and learning how and when to tell a trusted adult about bullying.

7. Teach the children the song, "No Bullying." It is sung to the tune of "Row, Row, Row Your Boat." If you wish, have the words written on a sheet of newsprint.

No Bullying Song

No! No! No! We shout! No! we shout out loud.

Bul - ly - ing, Bul - ly - ing, Bul - ly - ing, Bul - ly - ing,

That is not al - lowed. No!

Once the children know the song, teach them the A.S.L. (American Sign Language) sign for "no/not" as illustrated below:

Tell the children that they can use the sign every time they sing or shout "No!" in their song. Practice the song with the children using the A.S.L. sign.

Note: If you want to sing the song as a round—either here or in future sessions—simply follow the four divisions as indicated on the sheet music (see page 92).

Concluding the Session

Have the children form a circle around you. Set the copy of the No-Bullying logo poster on the floor in the center of the circle. Join the circle yourself. Invite the children to sing "No Bullying" while using the A.S.L. sign:

No Bullying Song

Ask the children to show that they "stand together" in ending bullying in their school by crossing their arms and joining hands with the person on either side of them in the circle, thus tightening the circle.

Collect any extraneous materials. Remind the children of the time of their next session. Tell them that at their next meeting they will hear an interesting story about what happens when bullying happens.

Optional Activity

After Step 2, read *Being Bullied* by Kate Perry and Charlotte Firmin to the children. Note, however, that sharing the story will easily double the time allotted for the session. Therefore, if you choose to use the book, plan on extending this initial session over two meeting times.

Session 2

Aim

To help the children define bullying, share ideas about bully/victim problems, and heighten their awareness of these problems

Objectives

By the end of the session, the children will

- define bullying

- share experience of—and become more aware of—bullying and its effects

Materials

- the No-Bullying logo poster from Session 1

- newsprint and marker

- newsprint sheet from Session 1

- posterboard

- pre-cut copies of the headband puppets (Teaching Masters 3-6)

- crayons or colored markers

- glue sticks, paste, or tape

- pre-cut strips of construction paper

- stapler and staples

- optional: scissors, one pair for each child

Preparing for the Session

Carefully read through the session plan in advance. With a marker or art letters, on a piece of posterboard, make a poster that reads:

BULLYING HAPPENS...

when someone with *greater* power

unfairly hurts someone

with *lesser* power

over and over again.

Note: You will need this poster for the remainder of the sessions.

Read through the story, "Ms. Skunk and the Garden Stomp," from Stories to Share on pages 59–63 of this manual, and be ready to present it to the children.

Make copies of the five headband puppets from Teaching Masters 3–6 (see pages 75–78 of this manual). Make enough so that each child in your class has his or her own puppet. Duplication is fine. Given meeting time constraints, it's a good idea to pre-cut the puppets. However, you could choose to have the children do this themselves. If so, make sure you have scissors available. From construction paper, pre-cut 2-inch by 14-inch strips, one for each child to attach to the puppets for wearing on the students' heads.

Make sure that the No-Bullying logo poster is displayed prominently in the meeting space.

Background for the Teacher

The heart of this session is the story "Ms. Skunk and the Garden Stomp." The story illustrates all four of the overall aims of the *No-Bullying Program* (1) defining bullying behaviors; (2) creating empathy for the victims of bullying; (3) the need to report bullying; (4) the consequences for engaging in bullying behavior. As a teacher, you need not point out all these themes to the children.

In fact, it is best simply to allow the children to begin to recognize them themselves—to let the story speak for itself.

Session Plan

Beginning the Session

Gather the children in a circle. Draw attention to the No-Bullying logo poster. Invite volunteers to recall what the logo means. Remind the children that whenever they talk about bullying *in class* they should not call anyone by name who may be bullying or being bullied.

Leading the Session

1. To introduce this session, display the newsprint sheet of the children's ideas, which you saved from Session 1. Briefly go through the material on the sheet, reminding the children of what they thought were:

   - the types of things bullying children do

   - what happens to children who bully others

   - what happens to children who are being bullied

   - how bullying affects their school

2. Display the "Bullying Happens" poster you prepared prior to the session and read it aloud to the group.

BULLYING HAPPENS...

when someone with *greater* power

***unfairly* hurts someone**

with *less* power

over and over again.

Take a moment to make sure the children understand the word "power." If you wish, offer some examples, for example, greater size, weight, verbal ability, and so on. Then go on to tell the children that they are going to hear a story about someone who uses power to bully. Before beginning, however, help the children quiet themselves inside and outside to listen to the story. Read aloud "Ms. Skunk and the Garden Stomp," which may be found in Stories to Share on pages 59–63 of this manual.

3. After reading the story, have the children identify some of the things Elephant did to the other animals. Record their answers on the newsprint sheet from Session 1. Look for responses such as threats, name-calling, loud yelling, stomping, etc. Compare these behaviors to behaviors the children have witnessed in school. Add any new behaviors to the newsprint list.

   Note: Again, save the list for use in later sessions.

4. Distribute crayons or colored markers and the pre-cut copies of the head-band puppets (Teaching Masters 3–6), being cautious that the children to whom you give the headband puppets of Elephant are not children who engage in bullying behaviors. Give the children time to color their puppets any way they wish.

5. When the children finish coloring, distribute the construction paper strips and the glue sticks, tape, or paste. Show the children how to center and fasten their puppets on the construction paper strips. Then have the children print their names on the back. Finally, help the children fit their headbands by stapling the ends of the strip together.

   Tell the children that they can wear their headband puppets for the remainder of this session and that they will be using them again the next time they meet.

   Collect any extra materials.

Concluding the Session

Have the children form a circle around you. Set the No-Bullying logo poster on the floor in the center of the circle. Join the circle yourself. Invite the children to sing "No Bullying" while using the A.S.L. sign:

No Bullying Song

Ask the children to show that they "stand together" in ending bullying in their school by crossing their arms and joining hands with the person on either side of them in the circle, thus tightening the circle.

Collect the headband puppets, making sure the children have their names on the back. Assure the children that their headband puppets will be returned to them when next they meet. Remind the children of the time of their next session and tell them that they will be acting out "Ms. Skunk and the Garden Stomp."

Session 3

Aim

To help the children identify and enumerate bullying behaviors

Objectives

By the end of the session, the children will

- act out bullying behaviors

- begin to discuss ways to deal with bullying

- create a list of bullying behaviors

Materials

- the No-Bullying logo poster

- newsprint and marker

- newsprint sheet from Sessions 1 & 2

- "Bullying Happens" poster from Session 2

- the children's headband puppets from Session 2

- covered containers: spice jars or cans, pill bottles, plastic bottles, etc.; one for each child

- soundmakers: rice, unpopped popcorn, dried beans or peas, salt, sand, fine gravel, etc.

- copy of the Bullying Behavior chart (see page 91)
  [For teacher use only.]

Preparing for the Session

Carefully read through the session plan in advance. Have at hand the newsprint sheet on which you've listed the bullying behaviors the children mentioned in the first two sessions. Make a "Bullying Behaviors" poster by dividing a large sheet of newsprint into three columns as below:

Bullying Behaviors

Hurting someone's body or things

Hurting someone's feelings

Hurting someone's friendships

Make a copy of the Bullying Behavior chart (see page 91). Review the chart prior to the session and have it handy for your own use as you lead the children through Step 4 in the session plan.

Gather covered containers and soundmakers (see Materials list above) so that the children can make rattles. (*Note:* If you feel making rattles would be too time-consuming or messy for your group, make each child a rattle yourself, prior to the session.)

Look over the Garden Stomp from the story, "Ms. Skunk and the Garden Stomp," and devise some movement and dance to teach the children. For example:

(Have children form a circle and raise arms above heads.)
First the rain, then the sun.

(Sway from side to side and shake rattles.)
Happily our work gets done.

(Stomp-march to the right.)

One for all,

(Stomp-march to the left)

all for one.

(Stop. Sway from side to side and shake rattles.)

Happily our work gets done.

(In circle, stomp-march forward.)
Come together.

(In circle, stomp-march backward.)
Have some fun.

(Sway from side to side and shake rattles.)
Happily our work gets done.

Practice the movement and dance and be ready to teach it to the children. Finally, see to it that the No-Bullying logo poster is displayed prominently in the meeting space.

Background for the Teacher

In this session, the children act out "Ms. Skunk and the Garden Stomp," which they first encountered in Session 2. Dramatizing allows the story to touch the children's affective states and helps them better understand bullying and its effects. It enables them to "act out" their own feelings regarding bullying, as well as begin to understand the feelings of those who bully. Make sure to alternate parts during the dramatization or to repeat it altogether to guarantee that every child gets the chance to act out a part in the story.

Session Plan

Beginning the Session

Gather the children in a circle. Draw attention to the No-Bullying logo poster. Then point out the "Bullying Happens" poster from Session 2 and read it aloud.

BULLYING HAPPENS...

when someone with *greater* power

unfairly hurts someone

with *less* power

over and over again.

Note: Keep this poster displayed in the meeting space for the remainder of the sessions.

Draw the children's attention to the newsprint sheet listing bullying behaviors that they created in Sessions 1 and 2. To help them recall some of the things they talked about that bullies do, ask:

What types of things do bullies do that make them different from other kids?

Remind the children that whenever they talk about bullying *in this class* they should not call anyone by name who may be bullying or being bullied.

Leading the Session

1. Tell the children that they are going to make rattles to join in the Garden Stomp they heard about in their last session. Direct the children to a work area. Give each child a container and access to the soundmakers you prepared prior to the session. Circulate to offer help to the children, making sure each has a rattle that makes a sound.

2. Gather the children in a circle again and teach them the movement and steps you devised for the Garden Stomp (see Preparing for the Session, above).

3. Give the children their headband puppets from Session 2. Choose five of the children, each with a different headband, to begin acting out the story, "Ms. Skunk and the Garden Stomp," as you re-read it aloud. As you proceed through the story, pause now and then to change "actors" so that every child has a chance to take part in the dramatization.

   Note: At the conclusion of the story/dramatization, be sure to involve *all* the children in the Garden Stomp.

4. After the dramatization, compliment the children on their acting. Then invite them to recap the bullying behaviors found in the story. Again, take care that any students who engage in bullying behaviors or who may be victims of such behavior are neither identified nor implied by name.

5. Have the children discuss how the different creatures reacted to the bullying behavior and dealt with the situation. Use questions like the following:

   • What did Little Rabbit do? How did he feel? (*Note: Be sure the children recognize how being the victim of bullying could make them feel angry, afraid, or upset.*)

- What did Orangutan and the other village creatures do?

- Did Ms. Skunk do something different?

- Was it a good or a bad idea for Little Rabbit to talk to Ms. Skunk? Why?

- What did the creatures do to give Elephant a *really* scary thought? What was that scary thought? (*He was not as big or as strong as the whole village.*)

- What did Ms. Skunk ask Elephant to promise? (*To stop bullying and never to threaten to stomp anyone into dirt again.*)

- Why do you think the village creatures let Elephant join in the Garden Stomp?

Conclude the discussion by saying:

> "Our school is like a village. No bully is as strong as the whole school.
> If everyone stands together, we can end all bullying here."

6. Display the "Bullying Behaviors" poster you made prior to the session. Read the headings aloud:

Bullying Behaviors

Hurting someone's body or things	**Hurting someone's feelings**	**Hurting someone's friendships**

Drawing on the children's discussion of the story and its dramatization and on the list of bullying behaviors they made in Sessions 1 and 2, list bullying behaviors—reading each one aloud—under the appropriate columns on the poster.

Afterward, tell the children that you will keep the "Bullying Behaviors" poster displayed in the room and that you will continue to use this list (and add to it) to help them deal with the problem of bullying in their school.

Concluding the Session

Have the children wear their headband puppets and gather in a circle around you. Set the No-Bullying logo poster on the floor in the center of the circle. Join the circle yourself. Invite the children to sing "No Bullying" while using the A.S.L. sign:

No Bullying Song

Tell the children that they can use the A.S.L. sign for "No!" anywhere or any-time they see bullying happening in their school.

Then, ask the children to show that they "stand together" in ending bully-ing in their school by crossing their arms and joining hands with the person on either side of them in the circle, thus tightening the circle.

Tell the children that they can take their headband puppets home with them. Conclude by reminding the children of the time of their next session, explaining that they will be talking about feelings.

Session 4

Aim

To help the children better understand and deal with feelings

Objectives

By the end of the session, the children will

- identify feelings
- discover how feelings affect them
- understand that feelings are temporary

Materials

- the No-Bullying logo poster
- "Bullying Happens" poster from Session 2
- "Bullying Behaviors" poster from Session 3
- one copy each of the "Happy," "Afraid," "Proud," and "Angry" Feeling Cloud (Teaching Masters 7, 8, 9, and 10)
- copies of "My Feeling Cloud" (Teaching Master 11), one for each child
- chalkboard and chalk or newsprint and markers
- crayons or colored markers
- scissors
- paste or glue sticks
- yarn
- paper punch

Preparing for the Session

Take care to read the session plan thoroughly in advance. Make one copy of the "Happy," "Afraid," "Proud," and "Angry" Feeling Clouds (Teaching Masters 7-10) for use during the session. Make each child a copy of "My Feeling Cloud" (Teaching Master 11). Have crayons or colored markers, paste or glue sticks, and scissors available for the children to use. Have a paper punch handy. Pre-cut 12-inch lengths of yarn, one for each child. To help the children memorize the poem (in Step 5), consider printing the words on a sheet of newsprint or making individual copies of the poem for the children. Be sure that the No-Bullying logo poster and the "Bullying Happens" and "Bullying Behaviors" posters are displayed prominently in the room.

Background for the Teacher

Although little children are not simply pawns of their emotions or feelings, those children who have not learned how to recognize and deal with their feelings are often at risk for developing patterns of behavior that can lead to bullying. It is crucial, therefore, to help children begin to recognize and name their feelings, and to realize that while they can't control the feelings that come their way, they can exercise control over the direction in which their feelings may point them.

In this session, the children discover that feelings affect them in body, thought, and deed, that is, physiologically, cognitively, and operationally. In their next session, they will learn that although they may not be able to regulate their physiological response to a specific feeling, they can control the way they think and act on a feeling.

Finally, this session helps the children recognize that all feelings are transitory. This helps children who may be experiencing uncomfortable feelings such as anger, fear, or loneliness recognize that such feelings will end.

Session Plan

Beginning the Session

Gather the children in a circle. Draw attention to the "Bullying Happens" poster and ask a volunteer to read it aloud. Then point out the "Bullying Behaviors" poster they made during their last session. Ask if anyone would like to add to it. Remind the children that you will keep the poster displayed in the room and that you will continue to use it to help them deal with the problem of bullying in their school.

Leading the Session

1. Write the word "Feelings" on the board or newsprint and have the children name some feelings they have had in the last week. Record responses. If the children do not mention the feelings *happy, afraid, proud,* and *angry,* simply add them to the list. Emphasize that all the feelings we have are fine.

2. To help the children discover how feelings affect them, say:"Every time you have a feeling, three things happen. First, something happens to your *body.* Second, something happens to your *thinking.* And third, something happens to your *doing.*"

   Then, to demonstrate how this works, give one of the children the "Happy" Feeling Cloud (Teaching Master 7) you prepared prior to the session. Have the child hold up the cloud over the group. Then say:

   > "Imagine you're at a birthday party. A very funny clown is there. He's doing wonderful and funny magic tricks. You feel happy, and here's what happens.
   >
   > "First, something happens to your *body.* You are relaxed all over; a big smile comes across your face; maybe your stomach feels all tickly.
   >
   > "Second, something happens to your *thinking.* You might think, 'Wow! This is fun!' or 'I wish I could do that trick.'
   >
   > "Third, something happens to your *doing.* You decide to laugh, or you decide to clap, or you decide to cheer."

3. Call on different children to hold up the other Feeling Clouds—"Afraid," "Proud," and "Angry"—(Teaching Master 8, 9, and 10), one at a time. As a child holds up a Feeling Cloud over the group, ask all the children to show what the feeling does to their bodies. Then call on different children to tell what the particular feeling makes them *think* and want to *do.* For example:

   - I can see by your body (face) that you're feeling proud. What does feeling proud make you *think*?

   - What does feeling afraid/angry make you want to *do*?

   - Is what the feeling makes you want to do something that is hurting or something that is helping?

Conclude by telling the children that in their next session they will learn a "cool" way to use feelings to do things that are helpful.

4. Display all four Feeling Clouds. Point out that all the feelings are in the shape of clouds. Tell the children that this is because feelings, like clouds, don't last forever. Feelings—even angry feelings—come and stay for awhile, but then they go away. Teach the children the following poem:

> *Feelings are like clouds.*
> *Feelings come and go.*
> *One day I'm feeling fine.*
> *The next, I'm feeling low.*
> *So no matter how I'm feeling,*
> *One thing for sure I know.*
> *Feelings are like clouds.*
> *Feelings come and go.*

5. Distribute copies of My Feeling Cloud (Teaching Master 11), crayons or colored markers, scissors, and paste or glue sticks. Show the children how to fold the sheet in half. Have them make the glad cloud face a cheerful color and make the sorry-looking cloud face a drab color. When the children finish coloring, direct them to cut around the cloud shape, fold so the two faces are back-to-back, and paste or glue the folded sheet together. Children who cannot manage scissors can simply fold the page on the dotted line and paste or glue the sheet together. After the children finish gluing, punch a hole in the top of their clouds, thread yarn through the hole, and tie the yarn.

Explain to the children that they can take their clouds home to hang on their doorknobs to show others how they are feeling—either glad or not-so-glad—depending on the side that faces out.

Concluding the Session

Gather the children around you in a circle. Set the No-Bullying logo poster on the floor in the center of the circle. Join the circle yourself. Invite the children to sing "No Bullying" while using the A.S.L. sign:

No Bullying Song

Encourage the children to continue to make and use the A.S.L. sign for "No!" anywhere or any time they see bullying happening in their school.

Then, ask the children to show that they "stand together" in ending bullying in their school by crossing their arms and joining hands with the person on either side of them in the circle, thus tightening the circle.

Before dismissing the children, remind them of the time of their next session. Tell them that they will be hearing a story about a way to deal with angry feelings.

Session 5

Aim

To help the children learn to deal with angry feelings and avoid bullying behaviors

Objectives

By the end of the session, the children will

- better appreciate how feelings affect them

- recognize how angry feelings can lead to violence and bullying

- learn how to express feelings of anger in non-violent, helpful ways

Materials

- the No-Bullying logo poster

- "Bullying Happens" poster from Session 2

- "Bullying Behaviors" poster from Session 3

- one copy each of the "Happy," "Afraid," "Proud," and "Angry" Feeling Clouds from Session 4 (Teaching Masters 7, 8, 9, and 10)

- copies of the illustrations for "Larry Lizard Lets Off Steam" (Teaching Masters 12 and 13)

- copies of "Letting Off Steam" (Teaching Master 14)

- chalkboard and chalk or newsprint and markers

- crayons or colored markers

Preparing for the Session

Make copies of the illustrations for presenting the story, "Larry Lizard Lets Off Steam" (Teaching Masters 12 and 13). Review the story (found in Stories to Share, pp. 64–66 of this manual) and note the directions for using the illustrations included within the story. Make copies of "Letting Off Steam" (Teaching Master 14), one for each child and one for yourself. Draw yourself in the figure outlined on your copy of "Letting Off Steam" prior to the session. Have crayons or colored markers available for the children. Make sure the No-Bullying logo poster and the "Bullying Happens" and "Bullying Behaviors" posters are displayed in the room.

Background for the Teacher

As described in the Introduction of this manual, there are two types of violence (*any word, look, sign, or act that inflicts or threatens to inflict physical or emotional injury or discomfort upon another person's body, feelings, or possessions*): **peer violence** and **bully/victim violence**. Both types are forms of behavior intended to do harm to another. Violent behavior tends to arise as a result of an agitated emotional state, most often frustration or anger. This session is designed to help the children deal with anger in a way that does not lead them into acts of violence, be they peer violence or bully/victim violence.

The children master a simple technique that, while allowing them to feel angry—a perfectly normal emotion—enables them to *think* calmly and to *do* something with their anger—to express it—in non-violent, helpful way. By means of the technique, the children learn that they can express their anger in a sedate and helpful manner (in an assertive rather than in an aggressive manner) or that they can cool off and allow the feeling—and the potential for violence it has triggered—to dissipate, to "pass," as all feelings pass, thus avoiding the path that leads to bullying behavior.

Session Plan

Beginning the Session

Gather the children in a circle. Use the rhyming riddles on the next page to review some of the feelings the children discussed in their previous session by reciting each riddle and having the children fill in the last (the "feeling") word.

I ran in the race.
My friends all cheered loud.
So when I came in first,
I felt really (*proud*).

We had a party.
A clown came named Sappy.
He did funny tricks.
And we all felt (*happy*).

The big dog barked loud.
It growled and it bayed.
The dog showed its teeth,
and I felt (*afraid*).

Sue promised to phone,
but she never rang me.
Sue broke her promise.
That's why I felt (*angry*).

Note: If you think it may help the children complete the riddles, consider holding up the appropriate copy of the Feeling Clouds (Teaching Masters 7-10) for each riddle.

Go on to display all four Feeling Clouds (Teaching Masters 7-10). Invite the children to recite the rhyme they learned in their last session about feelings:

> *Feelings are like clouds.*
> *Feelings come and go.*
> *One day I'm feeling fine.*
> *The next, I'm feeling low.*
> *So no matter how I'm feeling,*
> *One thing for sure I know.*
> *Feelings are like clouds.*
> *Feelings come and go.*

Encourage volunteers to tell about feelings they've had that have come and gone since their last session together.

Leading the Session

1. Introduce this session to the children by saying:

"Feelings just *are*. That means that all feelings are fine and okay to have. Feelings also come and go. That means that we can't always control the feelings that come to us or help what feelings do to our bodies. But we *can* do something about what feelings do to our *thinking* and our *doing*. We *can* do something about the way we *think* about our feelings and what we *do* about our feelings. We can choose to show our feelings in a way that helps, not hurts."

Go on to tell the children that you'd like them to listen to a story about Larry Lizard. Explain that Larry had angry feelings and showed them by hurting and bullying others. Encourage the children to listen well to discover how Larry learns to handle his feelings by showing them in a way that was helping instead of hurting.

2. Take a moment to help the children quiet themselves on the inside and on the outside to listen to the story. Read aloud "Larry Lizard Learns to Let Off Steam," which may be found in Stories to Share on pages 64–66 of this manual.

   Afterward, allow the children to share their initial reactions to the story. Then use questions like the following to discuss the story with the group:

   • What does your body feel like when you're angry? (*Have the children show you.*)

   • What does your face look like? (*Have the children show you.*)

   • Was it okay for Larry to feel angry when Alex called him names? (*Yes. All feelings are okay.*)

   • Was it okay for Larry to hit Alex? (*No*)

   • What happens if you let angry feelings push you into fighting with someone at school? (*Accept all reasonable replies.*)

   • When you're feeling angry, what else could you do besides fight? (*Accept all reasonable replies.*)

3. Conclude the discussion by leading the children in the "Letting Off Steam" trick Ms. Peacock taught Larry to do with his angry feelings so that he could show them in a way that was helping, not hurting or bullying. To begin, hold up the copy of the "Angry" Feeling Cloud (Teaching Master 10), then lead the children in the following:

   (1) When you're feeling angry, think to yourself, "This is *my* feeling. Now I have to do something to show it without hurting."

   (2) Take a deeeeep breath.

   (3) Let out the breath—let "off steam"—while slowly counting to 10.

(4) Decide what you want to say in a calm, "cool" way.

or

Use the "steam" of the angry feeling that's left in you to help you turn around and walk away.

4. Use the following scenarios to have different children role play "Letting Off Steam."

Note: Each role play requires two players, plus a third child to hold up the "Angry" Feeling Cloud.

- Yesterday, your mom promised you could go to play at a friend's house, but today she says, "No, you can't go."

  You feel angry.

- On the school bus, someone points at you and yells, "Wow! Look at that dumb shirt. You look like a nerd!"

  You feel angry.

- At recess, you get "out" playing kickball. A classmate laughs at you.

  You feel angry.

- You're working on a drawing. The person sitting next to you scribbles on it and ruins it.

  You feel angry.

Take time to process each role play by having participants share what being in the role play felt like. Also, encourage other children to suggest other ways to handle angry feelings by showing them in ways that are helping, not hurting.

5. Distribute crayons or markers and copies of "Letting Off Steam" (Teaching Master 14). Have the children draw themselves in the outline of the figure. When the children finish, hold up your copy of "Letting Off Steam" in which you've drawn yourself, point out the rhyme on the sheet, and read it aloud with the children.

> *When angry feelings come,*
> *at home or here in school*
> *I'll breathe real deep and count to ten*
> *That way I can stay cool…*
>
> *To say the things I want to say*
> *in a calm and peaceful way,*
> *or use the anger that may stay*
> *to help me turn and walk away.*

If you wish, help the children learn the rhyme by heart. Tell the children they can follow this rhyme to deal with angry feelings and avoid bullying.

Collect crayons or markers.

Concluding the Session

Gather the children around you in a circle. Set the No-Bullying logo poster on the floor in the center of the circle. Join the circle yourself. Invite the children to sing "No Bullying" while using the A.S.L. sign:

No Bullying Song

Encourage the children to continue to make and use the A.S.L. sign for "No!" anywhere or any time they see bullying happening in their school.

Then ask the children to show that they "stand together" in ending bullying in their school by crossing their arms and joining hands with the person on either side of them in the circle, thus tightening the circle.

Before dismissing the children, remind them of the time of their next session. Tell them that they will be learning how bullying hurts others and how it makes them feel.

Session 6

Aim

To help the children develop empathy for the victims of bullying

Objectives

By the end of the session, the children will

- increase their level of empathy for those victimized by bullying

- discover a way to prevent bullying themselves or becoming its victims

Materials

- the No-Bullying logo poster

- "Bullying Happens" poster from Session 2

- "Bullying Behaviors" poster from Session 3

- newsprint and colored makers (or art letters)

- copy of "Little Clarissa Cat Puppets" (Teaching Master 15)

- copies of "We Can 'Build Up'" (Teaching Master 16)

- tape

- optional: copy of the "Angry" Feeling Cloud from Session 5 (Teaching Master 10)

Preparing for the Session

Review the session plan in its entirety. Make a copy of "Little Clarissa Cat Puppets" (Teaching Master 15) and cut out the finger puppets. If you wish, add color to the puppets. Note the size of the puppets and that they are designed to be worn on *two* fingers. Carefully read through "Little Clarissa Cat," which may be found in Stories to Share on pages 67–69 of this manual and determine the best way to use the finger puppets to illustrate your narration of the story. Make each child a copy of "We Can 'Build Up'" (Teaching Master 16). On a large sheet of newsprint, use colored markers or art letters to print the following poem, taken from the story, "Little Clarissa Cat":

> Sticks and stones may break your bones;
>   we know that this is true.
> But names can hurt you just as much
>   so here is what to do.
> Put on a smile; speak true, nice words
>   to build up, not put down.
> Then others soon will call you 'friend.'
> Oh, what a happy sound!

Arrange to have a space large enough to accommodate the children's creating a "building" or "wall" of Build-Ups as described in Step 5. Have crayons or colored markers and scissors available for the children. Have tape on hand.

Background for the Teacher

While walking down a city street not too many years ago, a man noticed, in the distance, two young boys arguing. The man could see the boys, but he couldn't hear what they were saying to one another. However, their waving arms and pointing fingers suggested that neither was complimenting the other.

As the man drew closer, he could hear the little fellows' raised voices, but still couldn't make out what they were saying. Suddenly, the verbal barrage ceased. The taller of the two boys puffed out his chest and grinned broadly. The shorter boy's face turned crimson, and he looked as if he had been struck. He twisted his head from side to side as if searching for a weapon.

By this time, the man was almost abreast of the two verbal pugilists. He slowed his pace a bit and strained to hear if anything more would be said. He watched as the shorter boy recovered his composure, leaned belligerently toward the taller, wagged his head, and hollered, "Sticks and stones may break my bones, but names will never hurt me—you booger!"

Hearing this, the taller boy lost his smile and his poise. Tears filled his eyes. He turned and bolted from the fray crying, "I'm tellin' Ma!"

"Go ahead! I don't care!" the other boy yelled back. "I didn't even touch ya."

Names are just words, right? And words will never hurt? Not so. Words can be sharper than the keenest sword, more blunt than the heaviest cudgel. Why so? There are no innocent words. Words either heal or wound, build or destroy, comfort or distress.

This session focuses on the effects of hurtful words on a child in order to stress that not all bullying is physical aggression. In fact, studies have shown that besides physical aggression, bullying behaviors also include forms of emotional harassment, social alienation, and both subtle and overt intimidation (the latter often being—but not exclusively—the behavior of girls who engage in bullying). No matter the type, bullying is devastating to its victims. Children who are victims of bullying devote great energy to avoid being bullied. Nearly all their activity at school is focused on getting and staying safe. To end bullying and to help its victims, *all* the children need to learn to understand and empathize with them, so that victims will feel protected and safe at school.

In this session, the children learn to recognize bullying when it happens to others and to become more sensitive to their plight. Recognizing that since bullying is learned behavior that can be unlearned, the session also teaches the children a skill that will help them prevent bullying themselves and/or avoid becoming its victims.

Session Plan

Beginning the Session

Gather the children in a circle. Draw attention to the No-Bullying logo poster. Ask the children:

> What skill or "trick" did we learn to help us deal with angry feelings that might lead us into bullying? *("Letting Off Steam")*

Ask for a volunteer to step forward to lead the group in the "Letting Off Steam" activity. *Note:* If you wish, have one of the children hold up a copy of the "Angry" Feeling Cloud (Teaching Master 10) to begin the activity:

(1) When you're feeling angry, think to yourself, "This is *my* feeling. Now I have to do something to show it without hurting."

(2) Take a deeeeep breath.

(3) Let out the breath—let "off steam"—while slowly counting to 10.

(4) Decide what you want to say in a calm, "cool" way.

or

Use the "steam" of the angry feeling that's left in you to help you turn around and walk away.

Afterward, be sure to thank the volunteers for their leadership and the rest of their group for their cooperation.

Leading the Session

1. Draw attention to the "Bullying Happens" poster. Take a moment to review the definition:

BULLYING HAPPENS...

when someone with *greater* power

unfairly **hurts someone**

with *lesser* power

over and over again.

Stress that bullying happens whenever someone unfairly uses power to hurt someone else over and over again.

Then point out the "Bullying Behaviors" poster. Again, remind the children that whenever they talk about bullying *in this class* they should not call anyone by name who may be bullying or being bullied. Briefly go through the items listed on the poster to refresh the children's memories about some of the things bullies do.

2. Tell the children that they are going to hear a story about a little cat named Clarissa. Encourage them to listen to find out how Clarissa felt. Then take a moment to help the children quiet themselves on the inside and on the outside to listen to the story. Read aloud "Little Clarissa Cat," which may be found in Stories to Share on pages 67–69 of this manual. Be sure to use the finger puppets from "Little Clarissa Cat Puppets" (Teaching Master 15) to enhance your storytelling.

3. When you finish the story, allow the children to share their initial reactions. Then use questions like the following to discuss the story with the group:

   • How did Clarissa Cat feel when the other kids called her names and wouldn't play with her? *(Sad and afraid)*

   • Why do you think Clarissa felt that way? *(Look for responses that evidence awareness of Clarissa's sorrow and fear of being friendless and getting hurt.)*

   • If you think children your age could ever feel like Clarissa, raise your hands. (**Note:** *Ask one of the children to count how many raised their hands.*)

     Why didn't Clarissa believe the rhyme about sticks and stones? *(Names hurt her as much as stick and stones.)*

   • Do you think words can hurt and break others down?

   • What advice did Miss Turtle give Clarissa to help her have friends? *(Smile and speak true nice words to build up, not put down.)*

   Conclude by telling the children that they can do for one another what Clarissa did. They can help build up one another.

4. Give the children a definition of a Build-Up. Say:

   > "A Build-Up is something you say or do that helps others see what's good about themselves."

   To be sure that the children understand that they can use both words and actions for Build-Ups, ask:

   • What could you *say* to Build-Up others?

   • What could you *do* to Build-Up others?

   Then have the children pair up with a partner. If a child is left out, pair up with him or her yourself. Tell partners to practice giving Build-Ups to one another for one minute. Suggest to the children that they could say or do something nice and true about how their partner looks, the way their partner acts, or the things their partner does.

When a minute is up, have the partners discuss:

- How did it feel to *get* a Build-Up?

- How did it feel to *give* a Build-Up?

Conclude by telling the children to continue giving others Build-Ups. Challenge the children to give a Build-Up to someone they think could use one and then to watch what happens.

5. Distribute crayons or colored markers, scissors, and copies of "We Can 'Build Up'" (Teaching Master 16). Draw attention to the two building blocks on the sheet and point out the open spaces in each block. Read the directions on the sheet to the children and have them begin working.

While the children work, post the large sheet of newsprint on which you wrote the Build-Up rhyme prior to the session. Then circulate to offer help to any child who may need it.

6. When the children finish their Build-Up blocks, help them tape them around the poster you just displayed to create a "building" or "wall" of Build-Ups—be creative! As each child adds up his or her blocks, have him or her explain them to the group. When the "building" or "wall" is complete, consider adding the Little Clarissa Cat puppets to it.

Conclude by explaining that Build-Ups can help children who are being bullied feel better about themselves and get help to end the bullying. Tell the children that in their next session they will learn another very important thing they have to do get that help.

> **Note:** Consider leaving the children's Build-Up "building" or "wall" posted for the remainder of their sessions together. They will be using it again in Session 7.

Concluding the Session

Gather the children around you in a circle. Set the No-Bullying logo poster on the floor in the center of the circle. Join the circle yourself. Invite the children to sing "No Bullying" while using the A.S.L. sign:

No Bullying Song

Encourage the children to continue to make and use the A.S.L. sign for "No!" anywhere or any time they see bullying happening in their school.

Then ask the children to show that they "stand together" in ending bullying in their school by crossing their arms and joining hands with the person on either side of them in the circle, thus tightening the circle.

Before dismissing the children, remind them of the time of their next session. Explain that they will learn an important thing to do to get help for others or themselves in a bullying situation.

Session 7

Aim

To help the children recognize the distinction between tattling and telling in order to get help in a bullying situation

Objectives

By the end of the session, the children will

- define both tattling and telling

- understand the difference between tattling and telling

- recognize that they need to tell someone they trust about bullying to get help

- appreciate how adults in their school are willing to help stop bullying

- learn their school's procedure for reporting bullying behavior

Materials

- the No-Bullying logo poster

- "Bullying Happens" poster from Session 2

- "Bullying Behaviors" poster from Session 3

- chalkboard and chalk or newsprint and marker

- red, blue, and green crayons or markers

- scissors

- copies of the "Rattletail-Tattletale" picture book (Teaching Master 17)

- copies of "Stopping Bullying" (Teaching Master 18)

Preparing for the Session

Carefully read through the entire session plan prior to presenting the session. On posterboard, use a marker or art letters to make a two-part poster that reads:

> **TATTLING is talking to someone about a problem just to get someone else in trouble, to get my own way, or to make myself look good.**
>
> **TELLING is talking to someone I trust about a problem because I or someone else may be getting hurt.**

Make each child a copy of the "Rattletail-Tattletale" picture book (Teaching Master 17). Read over the story, "Rattletail-Tattletale," found in Stories to Share, pp. 70–71 of this manual, and be ready to present it to the children. Note that the *directions* within the story are simply referents to using the children's "Rattletail-Tattletale" picture book (Teaching Master 17).

Make copies of the poster "Stopping Bullying" (Teaching Master 18), one for each child and one for yourself. Complete your copy of the poster prior to the session. Be prepared to explain to the children the procedure your school has previously agreed upon for reporting bullying. Carefully consider using the two Optional Activities, making all necessary arrangements beforehand should you decide to do so.

Background for the Teacher

Tattling can be a big problem among kindergartners and first graders. These little people crave attention and often turn to tattling to get it from you or to divert it from others. Your challenge in presenting this session is to help the children recognize that it is appropriate to "tell" when they are being bullied or when they witness bullying, while discouraging tattling. An open and non-judgmental attitude on your part will go a long way in helping children "tell," not "tattle."

As you present the session, remember that children who are victims of bullying are afraid to tell. They're not so much afraid of getting a bullying child in trouble as they're afraid of getting themselves in deeper trouble with a child who bullies. Make sure that the children understand that you and all school staff are committed to protecting the victims of bullying and that any children reported for bullying will be watched by you and others at your school and will be held responsible for any further bullying behavior. If we're going to ask little ones to "tell," we big ones must be ready and willing to back them up when they do as we ask.

Beginning the Session

Gather the children in a circle. Draw attention to the Build-Up "building" or "wall" the children made during their last session. Invite the children to recite the Build-Up rhyme with you:

> Sticks and stones may break your bones;
>   we know that this is true.
> But names can hurt you just as much
>   so here is what to do.
> Put on a smile; speak true nice words
>   to build up, not put down.
> Then others soon will call you 'friend.'
> Oh, what a happy sound!

Encourage the children to tell why Build-Ups can help those who are being bullied.

Leading the Session

1. Tell the children that you are going to share a story called "Rattletail-Tattletale" with them today. Print the story title on the board or newsprint, read it aloud to the children, and ask them what they think it might mean.

2. Print the word "tattling" on the board or newsprint and have the children brainstorm what they think it means. Record all ideas on the board or newsprint, making sure to read them aloud to the children.

3. Distribute copies of the "Rattletail-Tattletale Picture Book" (Teaching Master 17) and show the children how to fold the sheet to make a four-page booklet. Tell the children that they can use the booklet to follow along as you read them a story.

Take a moment to help the children quiet themselves inside and outside to listen to the story. Read aloud "Rattletail-Tattletale," which may be found in Stories to Share on pages 70–71 of this manual.

4. Process the story with the children. Begin by eliciting their immediate reactions. Then ask:

   • What do you know about tattletales?

   • Have you ever been called a tattletale? If so, how did that make you feel?

   • How is tattling different from telling? *(Tattling gets someone into trouble. Telling gets someone out of trouble.)*

   • If someone accidentally bumped you and you tripped, would talking to a teacher about it be tattling or telling? *(tattling)*

   • If you saw someone bullying someone else, would talking to a teacher about it be tattling or telling? *(telling)*

5. Display the poster with the definitions of tattling and telling that you made prior to the session. Read the definitions aloud to the group:

   > **TATTLING is talking to someone about a problem just to get someone else in trouble, to get my own way, or to make myself look good.**

   > **TELLING is talking to someone I trust about a problem because I or someone else may be getting hurt.**

Go on to help the children better recognize the difference between tattling and telling. Present each of the following tattling/telling situations. Tell the children to give a thumbs-down sign if they think the situation describes tattling, a thumbs-up sign if it describes telling.

Should the children confuse tattling with telling as you go through each of these situations, gently correct the misunderstanding.

> Robbie Rattlesnake's brother, Raphael, kept tickling Robbie while they were watching TV. Robbie told his mom. *(Tattling: Thumbs-Down)*

> After lunch, some of the kids were playing tag outside the schoolyard fence. They were even running into the street. When Robbie saw what they were doing, he went right away to speak to a teacher about it. *(Telling: Thumbs-Up)*

Ms. Antelope said, "Don't open your desks while we're writing out your spelling test." But in the middle of the test, Butch Buffalo broke his pencil, so he opened his desk and got another one. Later, Robbie went up to explain to Ms. Antelope what Butch did. *(Tattling: Thumbs Down)*

On Monday, Robbie saw some older kids picking on Megan Mouse. On Tuesday, he heard the same kids calling her names. On Thursday, he saw one of the kids push Megan down and make her cry. Robbie went to talk to the principal. *(Telling: Thumbs-Up)*

Re-cap the difference between tattling and telling. Emphasize to the children that when they are being bullied and hurt on the inside or outside, or when they see someone else being bullied and hurt that way, **they need to *tell* a trusted adult in their school**.

6. Tell the children that they can make a poster that will help them understand and remember what to do to help end bullying at their school. Give each child scissors, red, blue, and green crayons or markers, and a copy of "Stopping Bullying" (Teaching Master 18). Point out the directions and read them aloud. Give the children time to work on their posters.

When the children finish, hold up the poster you made prior to the session and lead the group in reading it aloud:

> **If someone bullies me...**
>
> **If someone bullies you...**
>
> **If someone bullies anyone...**
>
> **This is what to do...**
>
> **TELL a trusted adult**

Take a moment to help the children *memorize* this rhyme. Afterward, tell the children that you will hang the poster you made in the meeting room. Then either arrange to hang the children's posters throughout the school or encourage the children to hang them at home.

7. Carefully outline for the children the procedure your school has previously agreed upon for reporting bullying (e.g., *how* they are to report, *to whom* they are to report, *when and where* they are to report, etc.). Make sure the

children understand that when they "tell" about bullying, their anonymity will be insured and that an adult *will* step in to help and protect.

Concluding the Session

Gather the children around you in a circle. Set the No-Bullying logo poster on the floor in the center of the circle. Join the circle yourself. Invite the children to sing "No Bullying" while using the A.S.L. sign:

No Bullying Song

Encourage the children to continue to make and use the A.S.L. sign for "No!" anywhere or any time they see bullying happening in their school.

Then, ask the children to show that they "stand together" in ending bullying in their school by crossing their arms and joining hands with the person on either side of them in the circle, thus tightening the circle.

Before dismissing the children, remind them of the time of their next session. Tell them that a special guest will be with them when next they meet.

Optional Activities

1. To enhance Steps 5 and 6: After Step 5, have the children print the name of a trusted school teacher or staff person on a strip of construction paper. Then use tape to loop all the strips to make a paper chain or "snake." Cut out a head and tongue for the "snake" from construction paper and attach it to the children's loops. After the children have completed their posters

(Step 6) Have the children march around the room, holding their "snake" aloft and reciting the poster's rhyme:

> **If someone bullies me...**
>
> **If someone bullies you...**
>
> **If someone bullies anyone...**
>
> **This is what to do...**
>
> **TELL a trusted adult**

Afterward, hang the "snake" in the meeting room.

2. To enhance Step 7, create a "Bullying Report Card" to give each child to serve as a reminder of your school's procedure for reporting bullying. Simply outline the procedure and have it duplicated on index cards or easy-to-carry sheets that the children can keep with them.

Session 8

Aim

To present school-wide consequences for engaging in bullying behaviors

Objectives

By the end of the session, the children will

- understand the meaning of consequences
- know the school-wide consequences for bullying
- better understand that all adults in the school are committed to making the school a safe and secure place

Materials

- the No-Bullying logo poster
- "Bullying Happens" poster from Session 2
- "Bullying Behaviors" poster from Session 3
- chalkboard and chalk or newsprint and marker
- posterboard or newsprint

Preparing for the Session

Carefully read through the session plan in advance. Prior to the session, use posterboard or newsprint to make a large poster entitled "Bullying Consequences." With the aid and consensus of school staff, list your school's consequences for engaging in bullying behaviors.

Note: Since the language of the school's "official" list of consequences may be too difficult for the children in your class, be ready to explain and/or re-word the consequences for them so that they understand them.

Arrange to have the principal in attendance to present the core of the session. However, since much of the Session Plan includes review of the past sessions, check it over to see if you want to make additions, subtractions, or changes. Likewise, a quick review of the stories you've shared with the children will also help you in leading the children successfully through this session. If you want to give the children an opportunity to "teach" the principal, consider using this session's first Optional Activity. Likewise, consider using the suggestions in the second Optional Activity. Finally, see to it that the No-Bullying logo poster and the "Bullying Happens" and "Bullying Behaviors" posters are displayed prominently in the meeting space.

Background for the Teacher

Even the youngest of children can understand the concept of consequences. Unfortunately, many children have experienced how consequences are not fairly applied. They need powerful reassurance that your school has no tolerance whatsoever for bullying and that your school will impose swift and strict consequences when it does occur. *Trust* is what is at stake here. The children need to trust that responsible and caring adults will intervene in bullying behavior and keep them safe.

Session Plan

Beginning the Session

Gather the children in a circle. Include the school principal in the circle, telling the children that he or she will be a visitor to their class today. Draw attention to the No-Bullying logo poster. Ask the children to explain its purpose. Afterward, invite the children to recall the difference between tattling and telling. Ask:

- What gets someone *into* trouble, tattling or telling? (tattling)

- What gets someone *out of* trouble, tattling or telling? (telling)

Take time to correct any misunderstandings.

Call on one of the children to read aloud the definition of bullying on the "Bullying Happens" poster. Then, pointing out a few of the behaviors listed on the "Bullying Behaviors" poster, ask the children to explain how someone who is a victim of that behavior would feel. Finally, have the children explain how they could help themselves or someone else who is being bullied by *telling* a trusted adult.

Leading the Session

1. Explain to the children that they're going to play a guessing game today. To play the game, set out a pan of water on a desk or low table and show the group the tennis ball you brought to the session. Tell the children that you're going to do some things with the ball. Their job is to guess "what might happen next." Use the following suggestions to play the game and add variations of your own.

   Note: These suggestions have you, the teacher, doing the action with the ball. If you wish to involve the children more directly, have different children do the following (e.g., *"If [Child's Name] throws the ball straight up in the air, what might happen next?"*):

   • If I throw the ball straight up in the air, what might happen next?"

   • If I let the ball drop from my hand, what might happen next?

   • If I throw the ball hard on the floor, what might happen next?

   • If I set the ball on the floor and try to balance on it with only one foot, what might happen next?

   • If I gently set the ball in this water, what might happen next?

   • If I hold the ball under the water, then let go, what might happen next?

   • If I hold the ball high above the water and let go, what might happen next?

   • If I toss the ball to (Child's Name), what might happen next?

2. Print the word "Consequences" on the board or newsprint. Read the word aloud and have the children repeat it after you. Explain that "consequences" is another name for "what might happen next." Point out that everything you did with the ball had a consequence.

3. Go on to tell the children that the things we say and do have consequences. Then, to reinforce their understanding, have the children recall

"what happened next" to some of the characters in the stories they shared in previous sessions.

> **Note:** In using the following questions, please recognize that the answers supplied are not necessarily the only acceptable ones. The children may come up with other valid consequences.

- When Robbie Rattlesnake tattled, what happened next? (*The other children called him Rattletail-Tattletale.*)

- When Robbie Rattlesnake learned the difference between tattling and telling, what happened next? (*He knew how to help others and get them out of trouble—not into trouble—and he began to make friends.*)

- When Clarissa cat learned how to build up, not put down, what happened next? (*She learned how to stop being bullied and to make friends.*)

- When Larry Lizard kept getting angry and hitting others, like Alex Alligator, what happened next?" (*He was sent to the principal's office and missed out on all the fun.*)

- When Larry Lizard learned Ms. Peacock's trick of "letting off steam," what happened next? (*He learned to show his anger in a helping, not hurting way, and everyone thought he was really "cool."*)

- When Elephant bullied the other creatures, what happened next? (*He missed out on joining with the other village creatures in the Garden Stomp. He had to promise never to bully, and his parents got told about his bullying.*)

If you wish, continue by asking the children to offer personal examples of consequences with which they are familiar; for example, ask:

- If you get into an argument with your sister or brother at home, what is the consequence?

Conclude by congratulating the children for remembering so much and for seeing the consequences of what we say and do. Then go on to tell the children that their principal will talk to them about the consequences—about what will happen next—to people who bully others in their school.

4. The school principal will now address the children about your school's no-tolerance rule about bullying and about the consequences for engaging in bullying behavior. Make sure the principal has access to the poster of consequences you prepared prior to the session. The principal should also

take time to reassure the children that school staff will support and protect victims of bullying.

5. When the principal completes his or her presentation, ask the children where they'd like to display the consequences in their classroom. Help the children post the list.

6. Briefly go through the list, letting the children know that you—and all the other adults in the school—agree with the consequences, promise to be supportive to children who tell about bullying and want to end it in their school, and pledge to protect all victims of bullying.

Concluding the Session

Invite the principal to join with the children in forming a circle around you. Set the No-Bullying logo poster on the floor in the center of the circle. Join the circle yourself. Ask the children to teach the principal their "No Bullying " song and to show him or her how to make the A.S.L. sign for "no/not." Then lead the group in singing and signing the song:

No Bullying Song

Encourage the children to continue to make and use the A.S.L. sign for "No!" anywhere or any time they see bullying happening in their school.

Then, ask the children to show that they "stand together" in ending bullying in their school by crossing their arms and joining hands with the person on either side of them in the circle, thus tightening the circle.

If you wish, conclude with handshakes, hugs, or applause. Before dismissing the children, be sure to thank them for all their hard work and their willingness to end bullying in their school.

Optional Activities

1. Extend the "Beginning the Session" section of this plan by giving the children an opportunity to "teach" the principal. Simply have the children give the principal a tour of the meeting room, pointing out and explaining the posters, displays, drawings, lists, etc., they created in their time together, and answering any questions the principal may have.

2. To help the students remember the "Bullying Consequences," make and give each student a copy the consequences on index cards or easy-to-carry sheets that the students can keep with them.

Stories to Share

Ms. Skunk and the Garden Stomp

One morning, Little Rabbit popped up out of his hole in the global forest. "Oh, what a very nice day to get my garden chores done," he thought. "I have lots and lots of long rows to hoe, so I better get started."

Little Rabbit had barely gotten two feet into the first row when he felt the ground beneath him shake. It gave him a queasy feeling. Then he heard the blaring of Elephant's trumpet as he came near.

"Hey, carrot-breath," said Elephant. **"You look pretty stupid with that hoe. I'm on my way to the village to round up everyone to come work at my place and make me a new garden. When I come back this way, you're coming with me, or I'll stomp you into dirt!"**

With that, Elephant thundered off toward the village.

Little Rabbit stood there shaking and feeling as if he were about to cry. He didn't want to go with Elephant, but he was scared. Elephant had stomped at other children before. In fact, Little Rabbit remembered how Elephant would kick others even when he was just learning how to walk.

Little Rabbit decided that he had better get an adult to help him. Ms. Skunk was an adult who lived nearby, and she was always ready to lend a hand. Besides, Little Rabbit loved the sound of Ms. Skunk's voice. So he made his way to her home, thinking about how nice it was to live in the forest near grown-ups he could turn to for help.

As soon as Ms. Skunk came into view, Little Rabbit cried out, "Ms. Skunk! Ms. Skunk! Elephant has been bullying me again. He says I have to work at his garden, and I have lots and lots of rows to hoe in my own garden. Would you please come over and help? I was thinking that if you help me, it would be ever so much more fun. The work would go twice as fast. And, besides, when Elephant comes back, you'd be there."

In her sweet and lovely southern way, Ms. Skunk agreed. "I've been meaning to spend some time with you, little friend," she said with a smile. "It's been a long spell since I was caught up on your news. Maybe we could work and talk at the same time. And don't worry about Elephant. We'll take care of him, too."

On their way back to Little Rabbit's garden, Ms. Skunk laid out her plan to have fun and to put an end to Elephant's bullying.

"I've got an idea," Ms. Skunk drawled. "Elephant may be bigger and stronger than you and me, but he's still young and has a lot to learn. When people are rude to others, no one really wants to be around them—much less work for them. Now we've got some quick work to do, little buddy."

When Ms. Skunk and Little Rabbit reached his garden, they gathered up all the noise-making things they could find. First, they picked up all the dried gourds from last year's planting. The seeds inside the dried gourds made scratchy sounds when they shook them. Next, they looked for other noise-making things. They found some old keys and nails. They found scraps of metal and old tools. All of them made tinkling sounds like wind chimes.

Ms. Skunk and Little Rabbit wired these noise-makers to as many hoes as they could find, so that the hoes would all make rattling sounds. Then, tapping their rattling hoes to a beat, Ms. Skunk and Little Rabbit, hoed the garden. Soon, they began to sing and do a stomping and swaying dance.

> *"First the rain, then the sun.*
> *Happily our work gets done."*

They were busy hoeing when they began to feel the earth begin to tremble under their feet.

"Oh, nnnnnnnno! It's Elephant come back to get me," cried Little Rabbit, his voice shaking like the earth.

"At least it's not an earthquake," Ms. Skunk said with a sigh of relief. "We can deal with Elephant, but you can't teach an earthquake."

It wasn't long before they heard Elephant's blaring trumpet. He was coming, all right. And he was driving a herd of young helpers in front of him. Soon, the village creatures, led by Orangutan, appeared. They were dragging their feet and looking very sad.

Ms. Skunk greeted Orangutan, "Hi, young friend. You sure are down in the mouth. You look like you just bit into a green persimmon that soured you up for sure."

"Well, I feel like I did," Orangutan said. "I got a powerful bitter taste in my mouth about being bullied into Elephant's work when I got plenty of my own work that needs doing."

"Then don't do it. You don't have to take Elephant's bullying," declared Ms. Skunk. Then she handed Orangutan a hoe and taught him how to sing and dance the Garden Stomp.

> *"One for all, all for one.*
> *Happily our work gets done."*

"All right, I just won't do it! I won't go to help Elephant," said Orangutan, "but I'd be glad to help you."

It looked as if Ms. Skunk and Little Rabbit were having fun, and Orangutan never could resist a good time. So he joined them, singing and hoeing and stomping.

The other village creatures watched Ms. Skunk, Little Rabbit, and Orangutan doing the Garden Stomp. They wanted to have fun, too. So they all took up rattling hoes and started hoeing and singing.

Ms. Skunk danced around, weaving her way through the crowd, strutting some fancy dance steps. She swished this way and that. Soon, all the other creatures were dancing the Garden Stomp along with her.

> *"Come together; have some fun.*
> *Happily our work gets done."*

They were having so much fun and making so much noise, the happy creatures didn't even notice that Elephant was standing and glaring at them. **"How dare you be singing when I got work for you to do!"** Elephant blared loudly. **"You're gonna be stomped into dirt, for sure!"**

Elephant was really angry. He didn't like the singing, and he didn't like the rattling. But most of all, he didn't like the creatures stomping while they danced. When they all stomped together, they made the ground shake! *He* was supposed to be the only one who could do that!

Elephant wanted to stomp somebody into dirt, but he wasn't sure whom. He really wanted to stomp Ms. Skunk, but she was a grown-up, and besides, he might never get rid of the smell. He was sure that the other elephants would tease him about that.

Elephant was so confused. He knew he was bigger and stronger that Little Rabbit and Ms. Skunk and Orangutan. Why, he was bigger and stronger than any of the other creatures. And then, he had a *really* scary thought:

"I may be bigger and stronger than any of them, but I'm not as big or as strong as the whole village!"

By this time, the rattling of the hoes and the singing and stomping were giving Elephant a headache. He didn't know what to do, so he decided to go home. And as he turned to go, he felt the earth shake a little, and that made him feel sad. He was being left out of the most fun stomping game he had ever seen.

Then, he felt a tiny tug on his tail. He turned and looked down at Ms. Skunk.

"Wait. Wait a minute, Elephant," said Ms. Skunk. "I need to talk to you. I know that elephants never forget, and you must never forget what happened here today. You must promise to stop your bullying and never threaten to stomp anyone into dirt again. Do you understand this?"

"I understand that nobody wants to help me or be my friend," whined Elephant.

"Exactly. That's what happens when you bully people," declared Ms. Skunk. "Do you promise to stop your bullying?"

Elephant's trunk drooped, and in a voice softer than soft, he said, "Yes, I promise, Ms. Skunk."

"All right then," said Ms. Skunk. "I'm going to talk to your parents so they know what happened here today, and they can help you keep your promise."

Elephant looked up and Little Rabbit and Orangutan were walking toward him. They were carrying a big hoe between them. Attached to the hoe was an elephant-sized rattle.

"We think that you could do the Garden Stomp better than anyone," Little Rabbit told Elephant.

"That's right," said Ms. Skunk. "If you stay and help finish up this job here, we'll come and help you make your new garden."

All the village creatures joined in. "We'll help, too. Please stay, Elephant," they shouted.

They really did want Elephant to stay. After all, *he* was part of the village, too.

They all joined together—Ms. Skunk, Little Rabbit, Orangutan, and all the other creatures—singing and dancing and hoeing and stomping. Elephant held his hoe and just stood there looking at them.

"Why, Elephant," said Ms. Skunk, "you can do the biggest stomp of all." With that, Ms. Skunk made up a new dance step that called for a very special, very *big* stomp. Everyone, including Elephant, thought that it was just perfect for him. SO, with a little coaxing, Elephant joined in, too.

That day, Ms. Skunk, Little Rabbit, Orangutan, Elephant, and all the other creatures in the global forest—everyone together—did the biggest, the loudest, and the most earthshaking dance ever—the Garden Stomp!

"First the rain, then the sun.
Happily our work gets done."

"One for all, all for one.
Happily our work gets done."

"Come together. Have some fun.
Happily our work gets done."

Larry Lizard Learns to Let Off Steam

Larry Lizard was not out on the playground for recess. Instead, he was sitting in the office of Ms. Peacock, the school principal. Larry was not happy.

"I felt angry at Alex Alligator. I thought, 'Alex, you're a creep!' and then I hit him," Larry told Ms. Peacock. "But it's not my fault. He called me names, and made me feel angry. I'm glad I hit him."

Ms. Peacock smoothed out her feathers and said, "Larry, you may be glad that you hit Alex, but are you glad that you're missing recess? In fact, you've missed recess a lot because of your pushing, hitting, and fighting with others. Are you glad when other children won't play with you because you might hit them? Are you glad that others say, 'Larry is always bullying. He's no fun!'?"

Larry didn't look at Ms. Peacock, but he shook his head no. Part of him didn't care what the other kids said. But a bigger part of him did care that he was missing recess and getting left out of the fun.

"I think that anger is like a dark cloud that comes over you sometimes," said Ms. Peacock. "Everyone feels angry now and then, and it's okay to feel that way. But it's not okay to use anger to hurt others. I think you need to learn a special trick of mine to help you get rid of your angry feelings without hitting."

"Well, okay," said Larry. "What's the trick?"

"I call it 'letting off steam.' The next time you feel angry, think to yourself, 'This is my feeling. Now I have to do something to show it without hurting.' Then take a deeeeep breath. Imagine the breath is hot steam, like your angry feelings. Then let out the breath while slowly counting to 10. By the time you've let out all that breath—all that steam—you just might not want to hit

anymore. Then you can decide what you want to say in a calm, 'cool' way. *But* if you still feel like hitting, just use the steam that's left in you to help you turn around and walk away. Try the trick, Larry, and see what happens."

Larry wasn't sure the trick would work, but he knew that he had to do something or he'd miss out on all the fun at school. He decided he would give Ms. Peacock's idea a try if he felt angry again.

On the playground after lunch, Alex Alligator came right up to Larry and snarled, "Hey there, slimy and stupid. I hope you spend every recess in the principal's office." Then Alex stuck out his long alligator snout, daring Larry to hit him and get in trouble again.

Larry made a fist. Inside, he felt all hot and steamy. He was ready to hit Alex. But Larry remembered what Ms. Peacock said, and he tried her trick. First, he took a deeeeep breath. Then he began to let it out slowly. "One…two… three…four," Larry counted, and he didn't feel so angry. "Five…six…seven…," Larry felt even calmer. "Eight…nine…ten," Larry finished counting. He felt cooler. He still felt like hitting Alex. But he didn't. Instead, Larry just smiled, and said in a cool voice, "See ya later, Alligator," then turned and walked away.

At school the next morning, Alex started teasing Larry again. But Larry used the letting off steam trick and simply walked away. Later, on the playground, Larry was having fun on the climbing bars. He spotted Alex and said, "Hey, Alex, want to play with me?" To Larry's surprise, Alex said, "Sure." They had a great time together. Then Carey Crocodile came over and said to Alex, "Why are you playing with Larry? He's always bullying and hitting everyone."

Larry wanted to hit Carey, but he did the letting off steam trick again, and he didn't feel angry anymore. When Larry saw that Alex was angry at Carey, he said to his new friend, "Just do my trick, and you won't feel be angry anymore."

"What trick?" Alex asked.

Larry explained the letting off steam trick. Alex tried it, and he wasn't feeling angry anymore either. Knowing the letting off steam trick helped Larry have a lot more fun. Oh, he still felt angry now and then, but he didn't let his anger turn into hitting. Larry knew how to let off steam. Everyone said, "That Larry is really cool!"

Little Clarissa Cat

Little Clarissa Cat was the smallest of all the animals in the school. Little Clarissa Cat almost always felt sad and afraid. All the other kids kept putting her down.

Every day, Clarissa asked Rebecca Robin if she could swing with her, but Rebecca always chirped:

> *"No, you may not!*
> *And do you know why?*
> *Cuz you're a little scaredy-cat,*
> *afraid to swing high!"*

So Clarissa would feel sad and afraid. Then she would arch her back and howl at Rebecca:

> *"Sticks and stones may break my bones,*
> *but names will never hurt me!"*

Every day, when Clarissa saw Freddy Frog hopping all over the jungle gym, Clarissa asked, "Can I hop with you?" Freddy just croaked:

> *"No, you may not!*
> *Besides, you can't hop.*
> *Cuz you're a little scaredy-cat.*
> *You'll fall and go 'plop!'"*

Then Clarissa would feel sad and afraid. She would arch her back and howl at Freddy:

> *"Sticks and stones may break my bones,*
> *but names will never hurt me!"*

Every day, when Clarissa saw Sally Snake zip down the slide, she said, "Oh, Sally, that looks like fun. May I slide with you?" Sally hissed back:

> *"No, you may not.*
> *You'll scratch up the slide.*
> *Cuz you're a little scaredy-cat.*
> *You skid; you don't glide.*

Clarissa would feel sad and afraid, so she would arch her back and howl at Sally:

> *"Sticks and stones may break my bones,*
> *but names will never hurt me!"*

Every day, when the other kids put little Clarissa down, she said her rhyme. But the more she said it, the more she didn't believe it.

"Names do hurt," she thought to herself. "Names hurt just as much as sticks and stones."

One day, Miss Turtle, Clarissa's teacher, saw her sitting all alone and crying. Miss Turtle sat down next to Clarissa and said, "What's the matter, Clarissa? You look very sad today."

"Do you know what, Miss Turtle?" Clarissa sobbed. "That stupid old rhyme, 'sticks and stones may break my bones, but names will never hurt me' is wrong. When I ask to play, everyone calls me names and sends me away. Those names hurt! They make me feel sad and afraid. I'm tired of feeling that way. What am I to do?"

Miss Turtle thought for a moment and then said slowly, "Well, Clarissa, you're right. The rhyme *is* wrong. Names can hurt a lot. When others call you names, they're using words to *break* you down and hurt you."

"So what can I do?" Clarissa mewed again.

"Well, you've already done something important. You've spoken up. You've used your words to tell me about your problem. Now you can use words to *build up*," Miss Turtle replied. "You can smile and say nice things to others. You can smile and say nice things about what they do. Just make sure what you say is true. When you smile and say things like that, you build up. And do you know what you build up? Friendship, that's what."

The very next day, Clarissa decided to try to do what Miss Turtle said. Whenever she saw someone, she smiled. Almost everyone smiled back. Wow! Maybe Miss Turtle was right.

When Clarissa saw Rebecca Robin on the swings, Clarissa smiled and purred, "Gee, Rebecca, you're really good at swinging. I bet you could swing right up to the sky."

"Uh, thanks, Clarissa," Rebecca said, but she didn't ask Clarissa to swing with her.

When Clarissa saw Freddy Frog on the jungle gym, she smiled and said, "Wow, Freddy, you can hop faster than anyone." Freddy thanked Clarissa, but he didn't ask her to play either.

"No one's asking me to play, but at least no one's calling me names," thought Clarissa to herself.

For the rest of the week, Clarissa kept on smiling and saying true, nice things to the others in her class.

At the beginning of the following week, something different happened. Sally Snake invited Clarissa to slide with her. Clarissa made sure to pull in her claws so she wouldn't scratch the slide. Sally was happy and called Clarissa her friend. Clarissa was very happy, too.

By the middle of the week, Rebecca and Freddy and others joined in playing with Clarissa and Sally. If anyone put someone else down by calling a name, Clarissa would say:

> *Sticks and stones may break your bones;*
> *I know that this is true.*
>
> *But names can hurt you just as much*
> *so here is what to do.*
>
> *Put on a smile; speak true, nice words*
> *to build up, not put down.*
>
> *Then others soon will call you 'friend.'*
> *Oh, what a happy sound!*

Rattletail-Tattletale

[Draw attention to page 1 of the booklet on Teaching Master 17.]

Robbie Rattlesnake uncoiled himself and stretched high in his chair. He waved. He hissed. He rattled his rattles. All to get his teacher's attention.

"Teacher, teacher," Robbie rattled. "Megan Mouse just took Ricardo Raccoon's apple!"

Megan handed the apple back to Ricardo, then turned to Robbie and gave him a hard look. "I was only playing. I was going to give it back."

"Yeah, that's right," said Ricardo to the teacher. "We were only playing until Mr. Rattletail-Tattletale butted in."

Ms. Antelope, the teacher, who always seemed to be smiling, wasn't smiling now. "Please keep your hands off what isn't yours," she said to Megan. "And Robbie, next time, if Ricardo has a problem, *he* can tell me, not you."

[Draw attention to page 2 of the booklet on Teaching Master 17.]

At recess, Robbie felt awful and wished he could just slither away. All the kids kept calling him Rattletail-Tattletale. Even when they stopped, Robbie didn't feel any better. He wanted to play, but no one would play with him.

[Draw attention to page 3 of the booklet on Teaching Master 17.]

The next day, Robbie didn't go outside for recess. Ms. Antelope asked him why. "It's no fun," said Robbie. "Everyone calls me Rattletail-Tattletale. No one will play with me."

Ms. Antelope thought for a minute and said, "Well, no one likes to be called names, Robbie. I'm sure that makes you feel sad and hurt. But no one likes a tattletale either."

"But if someone takes someone else's stuff or calls me a name, shouldn't I tell?" Robbie asked. "I tell because I want to help."

"Are you sure you *always* want to help?" asked Ms. Antelope. "*Telling* helps, Robbie, but *tattling* hurts. Do you know the difference?"

"I don't know," answered Robbie. "Maybe I don't."

[Draw attention to page 4 of the booklet on Teaching Master 17.]

"Tattling gets someone *into* trouble," Ms. Antelope explained. "Telling gets someone *out of* trouble."

"Tattling is talking to someone about a problem just to get someone else in trouble, to get your own way, or to get attention. Telling is talking to someone about a problem to get help so that you or someone else won't get hurt. Tellers make good friends. Tattlers don't have friends."

Robbie knew what Ms. Antelope said was true. Robbie promised his teacher that he would try to stop tattling. He really wanted to be a friend to others. He wanted to have friends, too. And he didn't want to be called Rattletail-Tattletale anymore.

Teaching Masters

1. No-Bullying Logo Poster

2. No-Bullying Logos

3. Ms. Skunk Headband Puppet

4. Rabbit Headband Puppet

5. Elephant Headband Puppet

6. Orangutan Headband Puppet

7. Happy Feeling Cloud

8. Afraid Feeling Cloud

9. Proud Feeling Cloud

10. Angry Feeling Cloud

11. My Feeling Cloud

12. Larry Lizard Lets Off Steam

13. Larry Lizard Lets Off Steam (cont.)

14. Letting Off Steam

15. Little Clarissa Cat Puppets

16. We Can "Build Up"

17. Rattletail-Tattletale Picture Book

18. Stopping Bullying

19. Bullying Behavior Chart

20. No-Bullying Song

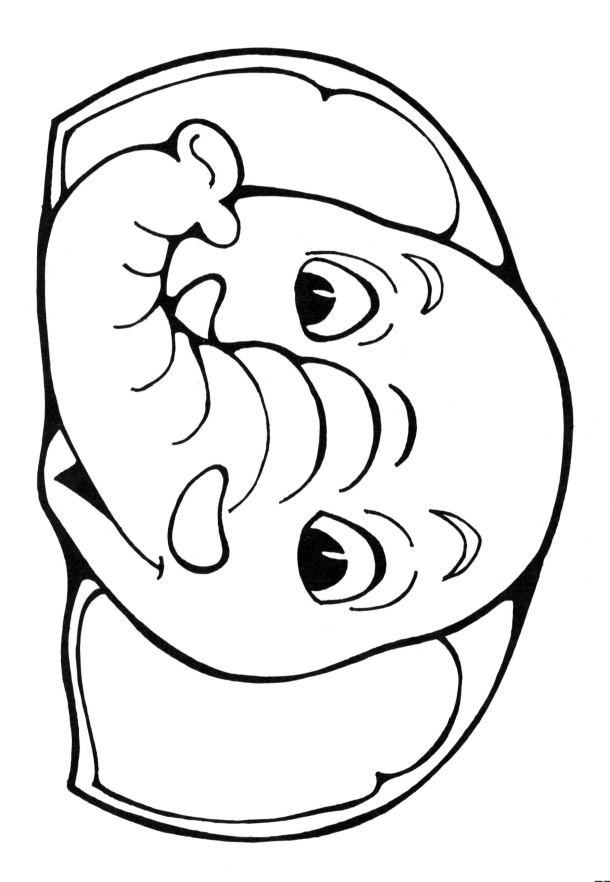

Teaching Master 6—Orangutan

FOLD

A

B

C

D

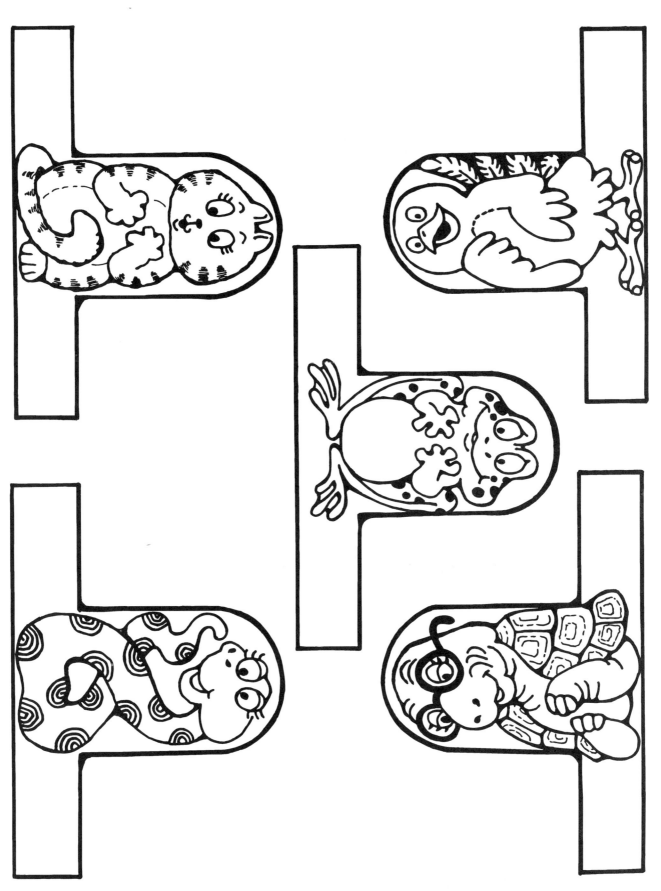

Directions: Here are two building blocks. In one block, write or draw something you could **say** to build up someone. In the other block, write or draw something you could **do** to build up someone. When you're finished writing or drawing, cut out the two blocks.

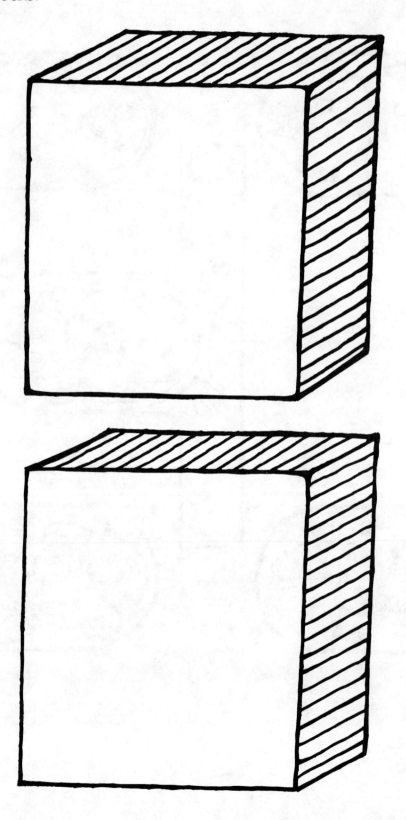

3

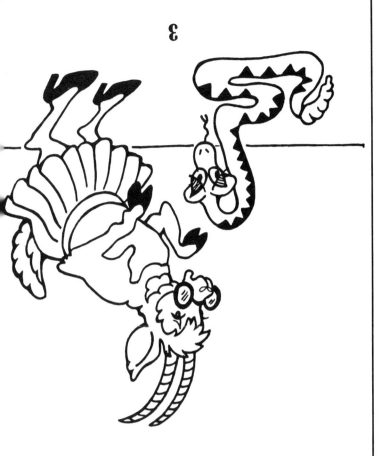

2

4

Rattletail-Tattletale

1

Color each shape with a ✱ RED. Color each shape with a – BLUE. Color each shape with a + GREEN. Then cut out along the dotted lines to make a poster.

Stopping Bullying

If someone bullies me…

If someone bullies you…

If someone bullies anyone…

This is what to do… TELL a trusted adult

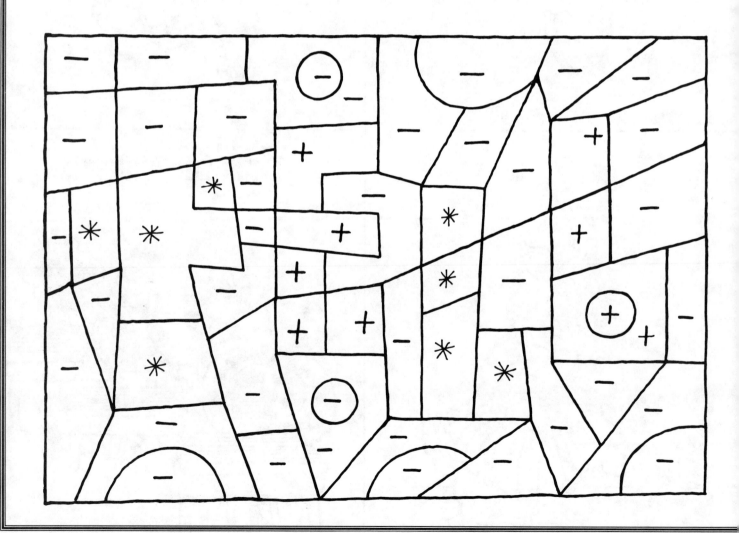

Bullying Behavior Chart

	Physical		Emotional		Social	
	Harm to another's body or property		**Harm to another's self-esteem**		**Harm to another's group acceptance**	
LEVELS	**verbal**	**non-verbal**	**verbal**	**non-verbal**	**verbal**	**non-verbal**
1	Taunting Expressing physical superiority	Making threatening gestures Defacing property Pushing/shoving Taking small items from others	Insulting remarks Calling names Teasing about possessions, clothes	Giving dirty looks Holding nose or other insulting gestures Saying someone has germs or is unclean	Gossiping Starting/spreading rumors Teasing publicly about clothes, looks, etc...	Passively not including in group Playing mean tricks
2	Threatening physical harm Blaming victim	Damaging property Stealing Initiating fights Scratching Tripping or causing a fall Assaulting	Insulting family Harassing with phone calls Insulting intelligence, athletic ability, etc...	Defacing school work Falsifying school work Defacing personal property, clothing, etc...	Insulting race, gender Increasing gossip/rumors Undermining other relationships	Making someone look foolish Excluding from the group
3	Making repeated and/or graphic threats Practicing extortion Making threats to secure silence: "If you tell, I will..."	Destroying property Setting fires Biting Physical cruelty Making repeated, violent threats Assaulting with a weapon	Frightening with phone calls Challenging in public	Ostracizing Destroying personal property or clothing	Threatening total group exclusion	Arranging public humiliation Total group rejection/ostracizing

Bullying involves exploitation of a less powerful person. There must be an unfair advantage being exerted. Bully/victim conflict is best understood as a dynamic relationship. Whether or not a behavior is bullying depends on its effect upon the victim. This chart was designed to assist with the identification of bullying behavior in situations where an unfair advantage exists. The seriousness for all levels of behavior should be evaluated based on the harm to the victim and the frequency of the occurrences.

No Bullying Song

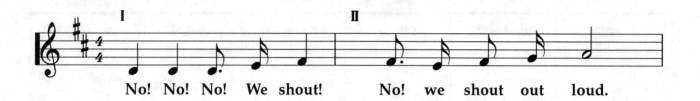

No! No! No! We shout!   No! we shout out loud.

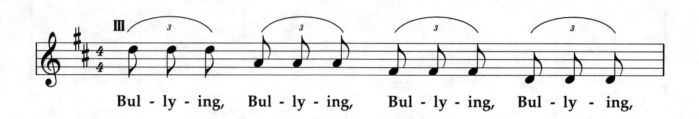

Bul - ly - ing,   Bul - ly - ing,   Bul - ly - ing,   Bul - ly - ing,

That is not al - lowed.   No!

Additional Resources

The following materials are available from the Johnson Institute. Call us at 800-231-5165 for ordering information, current prices, or a complete listing of Johnson Institute resources.

No-Bullying Program Materials

Tee shirts with the No-Bullying logo displayed on the front, posters, stickers, and extra teaching manuals for your school may be ordered simply by calling the sales department at Johnson Institute.

Video Programs

An Attitude Adjustment for Ramie. 15 minutes. Order #V429

Anger: Handle It Before It Handles You. 15 minutes. Order #V450

Broken Toy. 30 minutes. Order #V462

Choices & Consequences. 33 minutes. Order #V400

Conflict: Think About It, Talk About It, Try to Work It Out. 15 minutes. Order #V451

Dealing with Anger: A Violence Prevention Program for African-American Youth. 52 minutes (males), 68 minutes (females). Order #V433 (for males); Order #V456 (for females)

Double Bind. 15 minutes. Order #V430

Good Intentions, Bad Results. 30 minutes. Order #V440

It's Not Okay to Bully. 15 minutes. Order #5883JH

Peer Mediation: Conflict Resolution in Schools. 28 minutes. Order #V458Kit

Respect & Protect: A Solution to Stopping Violence in Schools and Communities. 28 minutes. Order #V460

Tulip Doesn't Feel Safe. 12 minutes. Order #V438

Publications

Bosch, Carl W. *Bully on the Bus.* Order #P413

Boyd, Lizi. *Bailey the Big Bully.* Order #P422

Carlson, Nancy. *Loudmouth George and the Sixth Grade Bully.* Order #P414

Crary, Elizabeth. *I Can't Wait.* Order #P431

———. *I'm Furious.* Order #P506

———. *I'm Mad.* Order #P509

———. *I Want It.* Order #P427

———. *My Name Is Not Dummy.* Order #P429

Cummings, Carol. *I'm Always in Trouble.* Order #P418

———. *Sticks and Stones.* Order #P420

———. *Tattlin' Madeline.* Order #P421

———. *Win, Win Day.* Order #P419

Davis, Diane. *Working with Children from Violent Homes: Ideas and Techniques.* Order #P244

DeMarco, John. *Peer Helping Skills Program for Training Peer Helpers and Peer Tutors.* Order #P320Kit

Estes, Eleanor. *The Hundred Dresses.* Order #P411

Fleming, Martin. *Conducting Support Groups for Students Affected by Chemical Dependence: A Guide for Educators and Other Professionals.* Order #P020

Freeman, Shelley MacKay. *From Peer Pressure to Peer Support: Alcohol and other Drug Prevention Through Group Process.* Order #P147-7-8 (for grades 7, 8); Order #P147-9-10 (for grades 9, 10); Order #P147-11-12 (for grades 11, 12)

Garbarino, James, et al. *Children in Danger.* Order #P330

Goldstein, Arnold P., et al. *Aggression Replacement Training: A Comprehensive Intervention for Aggressive Youth.* Order #P329

Haven, Kendall. *Getting Along.* Order #P412

Johnsen, Karen. *The Trouble with Secrets.* Order #P425

Johnson Institute's No-Bullying Program for Grades K–Middle School. Order #546Kit

Julik, Edie. *Sailing Through the Storm to the Ocean of Peace.* Order #P437

Lawson, Ann. *Kids & Gangs: What Parents and Educators Need to Know.* Order #P322

Mills, Lauren A. *The Rag Coat.* Order #P417

Moe, Jerry, and Peter Ways, M.D. *Conducting Support Groups for Elementary Children K–6.* Order #P123

Olofsdotter, Marie. *Frej the Fearless.* Order #P438

Perry, Kate, and Charlotte Firmin. *Being Bullied.* Order #P416

Peterson, Julie, and Rebecca Janke. *Peacemaker® Program.* Order #P447

Potter-Effron, Ron. *How to Control Your Anger (Before It Controls You): A Guide for Teenagers.* Order #P277

Remboldt, Carole. *Solving Violence Problems in Your School: Why a Systematic Approach Is Necessary.* Order #P336

————. *Violence in Schools: The Enabling Factor.* Order #P337

Remboldt, Carole, and Richard Zimman. *Respect & Protect®: A Practical Step-By-Step Violence Prevention and Intervention Program for Schools and Communities.* Order #P404

Sanders, Mark. *Preventing Gang Violence in Your School.* Order #P403

Saunders, Carol Silverman. *Safe at School: Awareness and Action for Parents of Kids in Grades K–12.* Order #P340

Schaefer, Dick. *Choices & Consequences: What to Do When a Teenager Uses Alcohol/Drugs.* Order #P096

Schmidt, Teresa. *Anger Management and Violence Prevention: A Group Activities Manual for Middle and High School Students.* Order #P278

————. *Changing Families: A Group Activities Manual for Middle and High School Students.* Order #P317

————. *Daniel the Dinosaur Learns to Stand Tall Against Bullies. A Group Activities Manual to Teach K–6 Children How to Handle Other Children's Aggressive Behavior.* Order #P559

————. *Trevor and Tiffany, the Tyrannosaurus Twins, Learn to Stop Bullying. A Group Activities Manual to Teach K–6 Children How to Replace Aggressive Behavior with Assertive Behavior.* Order #P558

Schmidt, Teresa, and Thelma Spencer. *Della the Dinosaur Talks About Violence and Anger Management.* Order #P161

Schott, Sue. *Everyone Can Be Your Friend.* Order #P435

Stine, Megan, and H. William Stine. *How I Survived 5th Grade.* Mahwah, NJ:Troll Associates, 1992. Order #P415

Vernon, Ann. *Thinking, Feeling, Behaving.* (for grades 1–6) Order #P250

Villaume, Philip G., and R. Michael Foley. *Teachers at Risk: Crisis in the Classroom.* Order #P401

Wilmes, David. *Parenting for Prevention: How to Raise a Child to Say No to Alcohol/Drugs.* Order #P071

————. *Parenting for Prevention: A Parent Education Curriculum—Raising a Child to Say No to Alcohol and Other Drugs.* Order #PO72T

ORDER FORM

<table>
<tr><td colspan="2">BILL TO:</td><td colspan="2">SHIP TO: (if different from BILL TO)</td></tr>
</table>

BILL TO:	SHIP TO: (if different from BILL TO)
Name _____	Name _____
Address _____	Address _____
_____	_____
City _____ State ____ Zip ____	City _____ State ____ Zip ____
ATTENTION: _____	**ATTENTION:** _____
Daytime Phone: ( ) _____	Daytime Phone: ( ) _____
PURCHASE ORDER NO. _____	TAX EXEMPT NO. _____

❑ Individual Order   ❑ Group or Organization Order

If Ordering for a Group or Organization:

Group Name _____

Please send me a free copy(ies) of Johnson Institute's:	❑ __ Publications and Films Catalog(s)
	❑ __ Training Calendar(s)
	❑ *Observer*, a quarterly newsletter

PLEASE SEND ME:

QTY.	ORDER NO.	TITLE	PRICE EACH	TOTAL COST

For film/video titles, please specify: ❑ 1/2" VHS   ❑ 3/4" U-Matic   ❑ 1/2" Beta   ❑ 16mm

SHIPPING AND HANDLING		
Order Amount	**U.S.**	**Outside U.S.**
$0–25.00	$ 6.50	$8.00
$25.01–60.00	$ 8.50	$10.00
$60.01–130.00	$10.50	$13.50
$130.01–200.00	$13.25	$19.50
$200.01–300.00	$16.00	$24.00
$300.01–over	8%	14%

Please add $8.00 ($10.50 Canada) for any videotapes ordered.

OFFICE USE ONLY
Order No. _____
Customer No. _____

❑ Payment enclosed
❑ Bill me
❑ Bill my credit card:

❑ MasterCard
❑ VISA
❑ American Express
❑ Discover

▢▢▢▢▢▢▢▢▢▢▢▢▢▢▢

Expiration Date: _____

Signature on card: _____

Total Order _____
(Orders under $75.00 must be prepaid)

6.5% Sales Tax _____
(Minnesota Residents Only)

Shipping and Handling _____
(See Chart)

TOTAL _____

Have you ordered from the Johnson Institute before? **Yes** ❑   **No** ❑
If yes, how?   **Mail** ❑   **Phone** ❑

QVS, Inc.

JOHNSON INSTITUTE®

7205 Ohms Lane ❖ Minneapolis, Minnesota 55439-2159
(612) 831-1630 or toll-free: 1-800-231-5165